LOVE, GUNS & GOD
in America

Christian Fennell

MONTREAL PUBLISHING CO.

The Real and the Imagined
Trilogy

Book Three

ISBN: 978-1-998353-02-6

Love, Guns & God in America/Christian Fennell—1st edition.
The Real and the Imagined, Book Three

Front cover art: Carolina Himmel
www.boutiquedeartedecarolinah.mitiendanube.com
www.montrealpublishing.com
www.christianfennell.com

ACCLAIM FOR
Christian Fennell's
THE FIDDLER IN THE NIGHT

"In essence, the author has created a work of art in word form."

- The US Review of Books

"Haunting and ethereal, Fennell's stand-alone *The Fiddler in the Night* is a masterpiece of reflection that is at once gritty, disturbing, and hard to put down."

- Midwest Book Review

"Fennell's haunting and poetic prose takes readers through the Godforsaken terrain of rural America on a wild ride to its stunning and heartbreaking conclusion."

- San Francisco Book Review

"At times *The Fiddler in the Night* is a thriller reminiscent of the dark, intense work of Cormac McCarthy. At times it's a coming-of-age tale, or a precise portrait of middle America. It manages to be all these things, while also telling an absorbing story. This is a cat-and-mouse tale set in grand, lonely landscapes and peopled with characters that feel achingly real."

- Neon Books, UK

"This dark coming-of-age story will impress readers with its distinctive writing and intense, at times violent, story."

- Booklife Reviews

Ce livre est dédié à:
NATHALIE GUILBEAULT
Avec amour et gratitude... toujours.

In writing this, I reach to thoughts of you, saying:
today, and today, and today,
for there is not a need of anything more.
Only this.
Only you.

"In time we hate that which we often fear."
- William Shakespeare

LOVE, GUNS & GOD
in America

Book Three
The Real and the Imagined Trilogy

Christian Fennell

PART ONE

In the coming of time; in the coming of love in the time of America, a man will lift his head from a thick and darkening pool of his own blood.

Hellish pain rushing forward, and he'll say, Jesus fucking Christ.

Dirt and gravel stuck to the side of his face.

There's a gun on the road, and he'll puke, mostly blood. A long line of spittle hanging from his lower lip.

Am I dying?

My kids.

He'll say, Isabelle, why?

And this man, everyone called him Finn.

Time here, time now, in America, and it's all changing.

Sterling Spalding, eating his breakfast on the terrace, thought, it's a damn good thing.

A damn good thing.

And let them hear this: Humble before God, praise the lord.

Fucking right, let them hear this, and let them hear it, always.

Through the barrel of a gun, or not.

He looked around, and he said, where the fuck is the jelly?

And now, time then, forty years back from time here, and Lizzy is down by the stream by the big trees by the muddy bank, and there comes a small breeze.

Buster?

In the shadows.

In the tall grass.

Buster Parker?

Lizzy. Zander's hand is on a damp stump and there are bugs and it smells punky. He moves away, closer to Lizzy on the other side of the stream.

I hav'ta find my bear.

It's by the big rock, I saw ya do it.

All the little feet sinking in the ever-mossy ground.

There's blood on her white nightgown, high up between her legs.

Buster?

And now a voice comes with the breeze, up from the downstream: You are a child of God too.

In the silence by the woods by the stream she is there. Why Zander? Why do we hav'ta go now?

I told ya already, ya know why. C'mon now.

A waxing moon in the still coming night. Watching everything.

Watching us.

In the quiet loneliness of this place, a broken, ten-strand post and wire fence, a small field with tall weeds, no livestock, no other sounds, big birds feeding on the easy downslope of the hill, a Shagbark hickory, long shadows of more time yet, and he said, hey, and he closed the door behind him, the wind rattling the thin tin walls of the drive-shed.

Looking at his younger brother cleaning a motor part at his workbench, Jake Burelson walked to the grease-stained fridge and grabbed a beer. He tossed the cap at a garbage can surrounded by empty auto part boxes, dirty rags, discarded bottles and cans, assorted other trash. What's up?

Looking back, his brother said, rings are broke.

Jake leaned his big frame against the tin wall and took a sip of beer.

What'd the doc say?

Said I'm shootin blanks.

Shit, Jake, I'm sorry to hear that. Have ya told Sugar?

Nope. And I'm not about to neither. Not tonight I'm not. He finished his beer and tossed the empty at the garbage can. He walked to the door and said, later.

Yeah, said Jared, later.

He walked forward in the coming heat, small steps in worn black leather shoes, baggy black trousers, white jacket, his bony papery hand with raised thin veins and dark aged spots lifting the Life section of the morning paper.

On his phone, Sterling looked at the boy, the boy's hand clasping his mother's long fingers, culled from this place and time, a certain form of thought.

There was something there, you could see it.

She didn't look at her father, walking past him with such ease and effortless purpose, slow, her bathing suit cut high over her high hips, her long brown hair falling over her bare back, much the same as the loomed broken dreams of this place; of our hearts laid bare before the coming of the moonlight. And now down wide stone stairs, a big white house farther back and high up. She stopped at the big pool, the clear blue water reflecting back the heat, the brilliance of white Hockney clouds rippling before her.

Ya play poker, don't ya? Sterling picked up a piece of toast. Good, we'll see ya tonight then. He flipped his phone shut and put it down and took up a knife and spread jelly on his toast. He took a bite and looked back at the Quiet Man in a dark suit sitting at a small wrought iron table set back from his and looking at the young boy still.

Finn'll want to stand. He won't be able to.
A long line of RVs driving by.
A young girl, pointing, will say, Momma, look.
Her momma will tell her, don't look.
But Momma?
Her father will say, tell her, don't look.
I did.
But Momma?
Tell her.
I did. Don't look.
He'll want the RVs to stop, but they won't, and he'll say again, Isabelle, why?

The man's bare feet find the dirty sticky floor, his elbows his knees, his hands rubbing his face and moving through his hair.

A father to the children, Lizzy and Zander.

Runaways.

From a father in the night.

He exhales to the late morning boozy air, and he leans back, his thin white chest and arms poxed with the markings of a man burning in the certainty of this place.

Of this heat.

He reaches for his cigarettes and lights one. He puts the lighter back on the nightstand and leans forward and closes his eyes and takes a drag. His body rank with destruction, and he knows it. But it won't always be. Not always. He opens his eyes and exhales, drifting blue smoke heavy in the hot dead air.

Lizzy and Zander walk in the woods, little and lost, the Spanish moss their covering. By the stream. Always stay to the stream.

Where are we goin?

I told ya already. I've told ya a hundred times.

Tell me again then.

California.

Oh, California. Is that far?

Yes, it is, it's far.

But I'm tired now.

They cross a dirt road and there's a thin old man with beautiful olive skin wearing a trilby hat riding a bike backwards. He looks and smiles, and Lizzy does too.

They walk on and soon they come to an open field. A young boy is there. He has long blond hair, long past his shoulders. He's short, maybe Lizzy's age, and there's a dog.

Looks like a wolf.

The dog looks back. The boy too.

What's your name?

Ty.

My name's Lizzy. Where are ya goin Ty?

Nowhere.

What'ya mean nowhere?

The little boy points south in the wide open field of that day, the beautiful tall grass, the sun hard upon it, a strong scent of alfalfa.

Lizzy looks to where he points and there's a small girl sitting in the moving grass, her back to them, her long full hair falling away.

Zander says, Lizzy.

I have to say goodbye to Ty.

Who's Ty?

Never mind. Goodbye, Ty.

But he is gone—and there he is, walking more yet down from the northlands, the dog out front.

Easy breezy, Lizzy thinks. Bye bye little girl.

She bounced her one leg folded over the other, a nervous energy of how she was hinged. Much like this place itself. Why won't you put that greasy thing down and come over here? Why won't you? There's no one here.

Jared didn't answer.

Sitting on a high metal stool she leaned back, her thin milky-white forearms resting on the workbench, her one leg bouncing, her thin summer dress high up on her long legs, and she tilted her head, the thickness of her blonde hair falling to one side and catching the light just right, and she knew it, and did so without having to.

She looked at her chipped red nail polish. Where the girls at?

Ellie stayed at a friend's. Alice dropped Addy at my mother's on the way to work.

Jake's working. Saturday or not.

Shit costs my money, Sugar.

I know it does. But he don't never wanna be at home. Not very much he don't. She looked out the small window. At the scrubby land. At the coming heat. Baby, it's gotta be time for a cold beer. This day is gonna be a hot one, it's comin.

He walked to the fridge and grabbed two beers and walked one to her.

She opened it and took a sip.

The fan in the window rattled and started up and it blew warm sticky air. He leaned forward, sweat from his forehead dropping to her thigh.

She looked at her leg, at the drop, and she put her finger to it, and it ran like a tear.

The smooth touch of her dress moving up. She pushed herself forward on the stool, just a little, just enough, a lazy southern cat stretching its underbelly to the warming sun.

Sugar.

I know, baby, and she looked back out the window. At a small bird landing on the outside ledge. Maybe a starling. She didn't know. She did once, when she was just a little girl.

A pickup will come, pulling off the road, a young kid with long dark hair stepping out and walking around to the back of it.

You got something to smoke?

You mean like——.

Yeah.

Right here, and ready to go. The kid'll fire up a joint and take a pull. He'll hold the smoke. He'll exhale, and he'll say, you look totally fucked up.

The kid'll step forward and pass the joint, and Finn'll close his eyes and inhale, the kid looking back at the big lights of the big town. Poor fucker, I wonder what the deal is? He'll look back at Finn. I'd take you back there, but I can't, I don't got the time.

You got something to drink?

I gotta couple of beers in the truck, ya want one?

Yeah, and Finn'll take another hit of the joint. He'll open his eyes and the kid'll be there, standing before him with a cold can of beer. Thanks. He'll open it and tip it back and try and swallow and it'll hurt like hell. He'll lower the beer and take a last hit of the joint and drop the thin stained nub of rolling paper to the ground. You need to be careful.

What the fuck are you talkin about?

A road like this can be dangerous.

Whatever.

I'm just sayin … and he'll watch the kid get back in the truck and start it up and wait to cut back into the long line of RVs. I just meant—and he'll watch the kid driving away. You don't always see what's comin next.

That's all.

What I meant.

He'll put his hand to the bullet hole in the back of his head, and he'll look at the blood on his fingers, and he'll say again, Jesus fucking Christ.

In the big space of the big kitchen there was only one small light on over the kitchen island.

Do you never go home?

He looked past the fringes of light, at Sterling Spalding's daughter, sitting at a small table beneath an opened window, the empty and the dark there, reaching far beyond her, this undercurrent of a restless stillness that is the South. There, wanting and waiting.

A darkened visibility.

The broken lines of her.

On my way now, said the Quiet Man. He looked at a large yellow envelope on the kitchen island. Can't sleep? He took a coke from the fridge and closed the door.

She stood and leaned against the end of the island, tilting her head, looking at the Quiet Man, her one hand moving down her neck, her long fingers of her other hand wrapped around a heavy crystal glass. She looked at a slow run of moisture on the glass. Not so much. She looked at the envelope. She looked back at the Quiet Man, knowing always the sense of him. Tell him to stay out of it. She leaned forward sliding her arms over the cool granite. I've tried. Maybe he'll listen to you?

His eyes lingering. And Hunter? Sleeping is he?

She stood straight and finished her drink. Fuck you. Just tell him.

And now Zander is tired, too, beneath a low heavy sky. The Spanish moss shaded, and it is weeping.

Lizzy stops, listening.

A sound in the woods.

What sound?

Zander?

Like a lamp held up to daylight.

Did ya hear it?

Zander says, shh, Lizzy, and he steps forward more, slowly, crouched over.

Careful, Zander, these bushes are prickly.

Quiet, Lizzy.

Don't touch em.

Look, says Zander, it's a monkey.

Sitting on a stump, there's an extremely large man, and he leans forward, slowly moving his massive hand over his very large, bald head. Turning, he looks at the children, and he tilts his head, his hand still there. He narrows his dark dark eyes. He smiles. A broad smile. A gold tooth.

Kurtz?

No, larger, but a killer of brutes, yes.

The Judge?

No, not judgmental, and kinder. Real.

God?

His son.

And he says, if I'm a monkey, I'm the Monkey King, and he laughs, a bigger than all the world laugh, in the wind, his harp music again, long and lonely, and forever still, over the sounds of the streamy water.

The children standing, looking, their eyes wide still.

The man lowers his harp, and he says, I'm not here to frighten you.

Zander, seeing all that he has been told, reaches his hand out to Lizzy's arm.

And you, Lizzy? What do you see?

She sees her duskywings, despite not knowing, if she'll need them.

Why are you two here? the man asks. In the woods, his long arms reaching out before him. In the dark.

They don't answer. Zander starting to back up, his hand still on Lizzy's arm.

I guess ya runaway, huh?

We ain't, says Zander. We're goin home now.

You are? And the man stands—the height of him, staggering to the children.

Yes, says Lizzy. We are—I mean, running away.

Lizzy! says Zander.

Lizzy looks at her brother. It's okay, Zander. We are. You're the one that said it. California, remember?

The man runs his hand slowly over his head again, tilting it again, and narrowing his eyes again. He smiles. His broad smile. His gold tooth. And he says, California.

He walks into the kitchen. There had better be some fuckin coffee. He picks up a small pot from the cluttered mess on the counter and looks inside. He puts it down next to the scrapings of burnt toast crumbs and he picks up another one and looks inside of it.

There's flies buzzing at the window, bouncing off the glass, and she comes, wrapping her arms around him, from the back of him, her sticky crisp blond hair in her face pressing to his back. Where are the kids at?

How the fuck should I know? Outside. Make some damn coffee.

Sitting on the porch step, his mug of coffee in his hand, his white and pink skin, his markings, his fear, not unlike all the others, there and for all the world to see, he thinks—but no, he cannot. Not that.

Lizzy.

Finn'll manage to stand, bracing himself against the rushing air of the passing RVs, the front of his white shirt ruffling in the moving air, the back soaked with blood. He'll tilt his head back and close his eyes and his equilibrium will drop out and he'll fall.

In the back pocket of his jeans his phone'll vibrate.

He'll try and sit and he won't be able to, and he'll dig his left hand into the dirt for a purchase by which to pull himself up, dragging his feet over the ground, leaning forward, resting his arms on his knees, his breathing slow and thin, his heart racing.

He'll try and stand, draining the last of his strength, increasing the pounding pain in his head.

Closing his eyes, he'll quiet himself, and in his mind he'll see the RVs stretching out on the road as far as his mind can see.

Mackenzie, he'll say.

Cael.

The fan high up turned the heavy blue smoke of their cigars, the light hard upon them, these aged and lined men with cards of fate in their hands. And they laughed. Why would they not? That two-faced bitch of God's lust far outside of their reach.

Fate boys, fate, and Sterling wins the hand. He looks at the man seated to his left. Come, speak with me now.

She wonders still. A man such as this. A Monkey King man.

And he stands, taller than us all, and where where is Lizzy's bear now?

Buster?

Buster Parker?

And who is ever to know such a thing?

The fate of invisible friends?

Sweating in the dead night air, his pudgy white hands gripping the balcony railing, he looked to the darkness, against the falling of a nation we came together.

What else could be done?

No, that's right.

It can't be stopped.

Not now.

Not ever.

Humble before God.

Praise Jesus.

He walks in the woods, his bare feet, his white cotton shirt opened at the neck, big baggy pants, a wide leather belt. He stops and looks back. Come along now, ya mustn't be staying out here. Not here.

They smoked more, looking out at the night, at God's own glory, the moon hanging before them like His own one bare bulb dangling above this darkened netherworld, reflecting the quiet flowing waters of the Tidewater River.

The shadows of big birds flying.

A warm breeze.

And these men; these types of men, freed from their worldly obstacles of wanting. But not their minds. That which they know to be true. An entangled magniloquent of thought. And we watch them, as we have through time, twisting in all four winds, and saying to the darkness, one nation within a nation under God.

These United Christian States of America.

What they wanted, and what they'll have.

Knowing always what the world needed—these gods, or the ones yet to come.

Guided by the truth of these hands.

Forever, and never letting go.

Humble before God.

Praise Jesus.

You can do it, Lizzy, go on now, you can walk in these woods, like that, with this man.

Come along, Zander, we can do it, we can walk in these woods, with this man, take my hand and don't let go.

And don't you worry, Lizzy, don't you worry one bit, we'll find your bear and keep it safe. We promise.

Everythin all right?

Finn'll look up and see a man with long gray hair tied in a ponytail turning his motorcycle off and setting the kickstand.

Anything I can do?

Finn'll try and speak.

I think your phone is ringing, can you get it? Where's it at? In your back pocket?

It'll vibrate again and the man'll walk around to the back of Finn and before he can reach into Finn's pocket he'll see a fresh line of blood trickling out of a small hole in the back of Finn's head, just below his skull to the right, pushing out past darkened blood mixed with bits of dirt and gravel. Fuck me, would you look at that. He'll see a gun on the road. Ya really fucked this up, didn't ya? He'll take the phone from Finn's pocket. Do you want it?

Finn'll look at the phone and fall from the heels of his boots.

The biker will catch him and help him sit upright. Jesus Christ, you're just about stone cold dead, aren't ya? He'll look at the phone. He'll look back at Finn. Can you hear me? Are you still there? I think it's your kids.

He'd like to stand.

What'ya want me to do?

But he can't.

It's from Mackenzie. Would ya like me to read it?

He'd like the RVs to stop.

She says, hey Dad, Cael's with me, we're here for the call. Dad? Are you there?

But they won't.

She wants to know if you're still coming home for her graduation. She says, it's in two weeks.

The phone'll vibrate again and the biker will look. He'll pause, not wanting to read anymore. Not wanting anymore of these shitty reminders. He'll place the phone on Finn's lap. It's there if you want it, and he'll say, look, I'll tell ya what, I'll call 911, but that's it, that's all I can do. They won't get here for a while, but at least you won't be left out here dead at the side of the road.

He'll walk back to his bike and take his phone from his jacket pocket and make the call. He'll give his name and the reason for his call and hang up. He'll put his phone away and he'll look back at Finn. Listen, brother, I'm sorry about your troubles, I really am, but I gotta go. He'll start the bike up and take it off the kickstand and ride down the side of the road, tucking in behind an RV, disappearing back into the long line of their conformity that rolls on over these high hills without trees in perfect sync and harmony until fading away somewhere just beyond the farthest reaches of the midnight sun.

Did he pick up?

No, Mackenzie will tell her younger brother, Cael. But he had better come home soon, I can tell you that much.

Cael'll turn and walk away, and she'll watch her brother go, standing there in the quiet empty of a parking lot next to an old brick wall of a small building. A café. A bakery. Finley's Home Hardware. Tidewater. Early, the sun just up over a small town.

He'll walk more yet, just eleven-years-old, out past the broken pavement, across the scrubby weeds and the tall grass section of flat land, and into the woods. He'll climb an embankment and walk until he comes to a set of railroad tracks where he likes to go, the heavy air turning before him, stepping over sticky creosote and wayward stones. He'll come to a bend where the trees stop and he can see the town. A town he did not know. Did not care to know. And why would he? And where the hell are you? And why won't you come home? He'll look back at the big white house atop of that high hill and all the other nice houses coming down from there, the road dropping toward town, to the river, and its tidewater, the one bridge to all the other houses, moving on until you got closer to the mill where his dad once worked when he was just young. He'll pick up a stone and throw it at the river. The hell with you, we miss her, too, you know.

He'll come back.

The two of them looking out from the back door, a tall thin old man with white hair, a faded green apron with the word Finley's on the front, and that young girl, just thirteen, and so big now, looking up with big round brown eyes and long dark hair. Worlds apart, this suggestion of us. In a look. An opened back door. Quiet on a Saturday morning.

What'ya say we get the sign out and the door opened up, their grandfather will say to them. You go on and I'll just stand here and worry him home a bit more.

PART TWO

The older model mountain truck pulled off the road and stopped and Finn threw his bag to the side of the road and jumped out. He watched the truck driving away, and he picked up his bag, and he walked toward the town.

There was still one contract to go, but he'd had enough. Three months of planting trees in the mountains was more than enough, especially at his age, pushing fifty. The others, all being eighteen to twenty-six, were mostly all right, especially once they had gotten used to having an older guy in camp.

The truth was, he missed his kids too much. He missed them every day, and he wanted nothing more than to be back there with them now.

He'd been no good to them before he left, he knew that, and he'd hoped this might change things.

Did it?

He wasn't sure.

He found a laundromat and loaded his clothes into a machine. He stepped outside and checked his watch.

He opened the door of a general store and walked to the back. He bought two cold beers and a green apple.

He sat on a bench in the town square and drank his beer and ate his apple and he wondered. In the church of our knowing, the blood runs, it always runs, in the streets of our towns, and the streets of our hearts.

He shaded his eyes to the rim of the sun low in the sky before him. There was an old man there with a shopping cart, stopped, smoking down a cigarette, looking off somewhere else.

He wondered more, and he thought, you were to stay in your rooms, but you didn't, you came to the door.

Why?

Bye, Mom.

I told em, in the dark, in the cold, she can't hear you, your head, Lizzy, bouncing against my back, your long hair hanging down, your wrists bandaged, little emptied plastic bottles jangling in my pockets.

Beyond the intensity of the darkness of that night, these real nights of us, there was no road to follow.

You slept for two days and your heart didn't stop.

We knew the storm was coming and I had only just beat it out getting into town and back to get some things we needed.

I gave you your pill and waited until you were out.

It was one of those times it didn't work.

You were sitting on the couch with the kids watching a movie, both wrists opened up, two puddles of blood on the floor.

She's been talking gibberish.

What is madness and how did it find us? A last glimpse of our diminishing reality. A last chance to reach out and find some handles and hold on.

For how long?

Fight harder.

Be stronger.

A weakness in the heart of knowing, so much of everyone's truth.

He took another sip of beer and stretched his legs out and crossed his boots and in his mind he searched for her more.

His wife.

Then.

He felt the essence of her still. Her scent. Her touch. All that he wanted again right now, covering him—that calming.

Lizzy.

Just like it was yesterday.

That's what he thought, and often wished he didn't.

And he found her now, sitting on the porch stairs, the sun warming on her face, watching the kids walking down the long, shaded driveway. Walking and talking, playing, stopping to see the horses come to the post and rail fence to see them off. The horses' tails flicking at flies, the school bus honking and waiting.

You wore faded and ripped jeans, a white tank top, and we stretched back to the warm porch boards and made love in the sunlight.

We smoked and we talked, time passing in our words like a faint breeze across our world—a world no longer ours in the making. The fog in your brain coming, going away, coming back, and settling again.

And it couldn't be stopped.

Not by me, the doctors, meds, not by the letting of your own blood.

It would come.

He finished his beer and took the other one from his pocket and opened it.

Like the lily and the rose.

Je me souviens.

Like it never will be again.

He looked across the blurred square. We were always together, though, weren't we, Lizzy? Even then. Always then. Reaching to that one same sun, same big sky, sheltering us, lazy and lingering in the tall grass by the big shady river. The purity of your heart bringing to us the rhythm of everything good.

Forever.

That's what we thought.

And never not just like that.

He looked at the store that sold the beer. It was closed. He took another sip of beer and leaned forward and put his finger to the dirt and wrote the words, In the wind: A refrain.

He spat to the dirt and lit a cigarette.

That night.

You drank a bottle of red wine, and you took another one with you, and you drove away. You drove down a dark country road and you drove onto an irrigated field of beans and you ran a jagged piece of green glass across your wrists.

They said you wouldn't make it. But you did. You stayed.

He shook the match out and tossed it to the ground, and he thought about that, what it must have been like, stopped, all that emptiness and darkness coming and settling upon you.

In the dark.

In the quiet.

Waiting.

He took a drag of his cigarette and kicked dirt onto the smouldering match. You wrote a note in red ink on the back of a cigarette pack, and I couldn't make it out, what it is you wrote. Not really.

He looked at the old man, stopped, looking back at him.

That was the hardest part, wasn't it? That knowing. The slash and burn of so many sharp declines, the going heavy in the darkness, and always there waiting, the certainty of it coming, with little to do but try and make it through.

He took a drag of his cigarette and dropped it to the ground and toed it out. You woke from a late morning nap and walked to the window, watching for a while, crisp red-brown leaves whirling and tumbling down the vacant road.

You looked at me, and I could see it, the very same as if it were an object you held in your hands before me. Your wellness had surrendered, betraying you again, our hopes held tight beneath warm sheets in the night—gone. Fallen away again.

He heard the old man's cart start up with its one squeaky wheel and he watched him push it down a narrow shaded laneway.

Blood on the sheets, on the curtains, on the floor, and down the hallway.

An altered state that became a constant, and it shouldn't have been.

There were no other options.

Why?

It's a good question, one you can hold up to the light and never be satisfied with what the reflections of you are trying to see.

An unrelenting death repetitiveness that you and your children could not stop.

They'd wash your current meds out and start a new round, something different. Anything. But it wouldn't hold, it never did.

He watched the old man disappear, the squeak of the wheel still coming to him like some demented whistle moving over the empty courtyard and settling before him. He leaned forward, his hand open to it, grabbing hold of it, and it made him feel better, choking the calling of it until it was rung out and gone. He opened his hand and dropped the deadness of it to the ground.

Just like you, Lizzy.

Dead and gone.

Once everything had failed, every possible combination of meds, all those rounds of ECT, everything changed, the being diagnosed as Treatment Resistant became a divide. The four to six week stays in the hospital, being moved to a university hospital specializing in mental disorders and studied for three months, it all stopped.

We so easily sacrifice science to the altar of our beliefs, and yet, we hide behind it, too, filling voids, segregating ourselves. Scapegoating. Because if we didn't, we'd be forced to examine the other side of us, the collective side, the uncomfortable truth that it is all of us together.

One in five, how could it not be?

Locked in cold dead rooms with restraints, looking at you through heavy glass.

Little harmless beautiful you.

"I can show you how to kill yourself, if you really want to die."

That's what the nurse said, Lizzy, and I asked her, why? Why would you say that?

You were taking up a bed someone who wants to live could use.

Imagine that, Lizzy? But all too true and far too prevalent.

You escaped triage, broke out and ran, over Fiddler's Green, picked up in the night by the police, and it did not matter if it was the hospital you fled because you needed to be there, you were charged and arrested and set free in the morning to the world, barefoot.

He took another sip of beer and thought, I really don't care who you are, how old you are, your understandings, your beliefs, lack of them, healthcare professional, or not, family, or not— take your bootstraps and keep walking.

He looked again in the direction of the squeaky wheel sound that was not there now, the square lonelier for its absence, the stillness and silence heavier.

We'd moved to that little house in town, and I went down into the basement. I can't remember why. I've tried. Over and over, I've tried. I came back up and you were gone. And it wasn't like before, there were too many places now for you to go that I did not know. Too many side streets, dead-ends, parks, and strip malls.

They found you.

Not me.

Not that time.

Alone again in the night, parked behind an empty building.

Why that?

Always that?

Did I do it? Put that there? Empty bottles squeezed tight at your feet.

I couldn't do it, be your witness, and I'm sorry about that, even though you wanted me to.

No one was stronger, fought harder, or longer. Not that I know of. And you deserved that witness, and I guess I was that, just not how you needed me to be.

Not in the end I wasn't.

Where's that sound, old man? Bring it back. Break the emptiness, and I'll be your witness and you be mine.

He looked at the sun, almost gone and taking everything with it.

Lizzy?

Bravery is caring. It's understanding the weakness in the heart of all our truth and still caring.

Lizzy?

And I wonder if you can understand that?

Can you?

I'm right here, Finn.

I sat in the car one time, did you know that?

No. When?

You were in the backseat all torn up, and I didn't drive, not right away I didn't. I just sat there, wanting to yell—scream, so fucking loud. But who was there to hear me? That's what I didn't know.

There was no one, that's who.

What about God? he heard Lizzy say to him, and he turned and looked in the direction of the old man wearing the trilby hat who was not there now.

Her voice coming to him again. Finn, what would you of said to Him?

I don't know, Lizzy. I guess I would've said, hold on, what's going on?

And what would He of said?

Finn looked at the coming darkness and thought, healthcare for humanity, how hard can that be to understand? Love and caring, Lizzy, that's what He'd of said.

Yes, Finn, love and caring. It's all we have and all that's required.

No, Lizzy, all we have is the cold hard reach of science, new meds and go home.

And now the old man was there, standing next to him, and he thought, how'd you get there? And he thought, where's Lizzy? Where'd she go? Lizzy?

He watched the old man tip his head back and close his eyes, scenting the coming winds, much the same as a dog might do.

He looked at the low dark clouds moving quickly above him, the old man disappearing again across the darkening square, the sound of the squeaky wheel drifting and fading with the falling sun.

Will it never stop?

Say goodbye.

No, not today.

Say goodbye. It's all that's left.

He heard a cricket and he looked to a patch of dead weeds coming up from the dirt. He leaned his head back and closed his eyes and let the coming darkness take him, and it did, and in his mind, he ran, once again, the dark and empty streets of our hearts.

He felt a warm breeze, a light touch, a whispering: In the guardianship of perfect silence all shall be known.

He opened his eyes, unable to distinguish himself from his wanting, from that which was there, real or imagined. From the darkness they had known together. Her eyes before him now, so clear and blue, her long black hair, red lips—dancing, together, under the moonlight, over the empty courtyard. As if touched as one by the stain of this life.

The old man, farther down in the square, stopping and looking back at Finn. All alone.

In the dark.

In the quiet.

Waiting.

Why do you always gotta come here? Mackenzie's irritation at the stones on the railway ties clear. There's nothing here.

Cael didn't answer and he tried to ignore her.

You can't just come here and do nothing. We ain't gettin stuck in this place.

He looked at his sister. He said he's coming home.

What if he doesn't?

Well, he said he was.

I know what he said, but somethin always comes up, doesn't it?

He'll come home, said Cael.

He'd better, and Mackenzie looked, too, at the lazy rolling river cutting through the lowlands and tall grass, big birds coming to the heavy hanging branches with their Spanish moss.

The two of them just looking, and not knowing, and hoping, and maybe he would come home?

Let's call him, said Mackenzie.

Should we?

Of course, we should.

We could try.

I'm gonna do it right now.

Finn's phone ran and he answered it.

Dad?

Hi, Kenzie. Is Cael there with you?

Yeah. Dad?

Yeah.

Just so you know, I will not be going shopping for a grad dress with Grandmother, which I am more than sure she thinks is happening. Do you understand?

I understand. Have you been helping your grandfather at the store? What about Cael?

Dad?

Yeah, fine, what do you want me to do about it?

Cael held his hand out. Let me speak to him.

Mackenzie's hand shot up to her brother's face. I want you to come home is what I want you to do, right now, and take me to buy a dress, which, by the way, will not be here, in this pathetic little place.

I finished my last contract yesterday. I'll be on a bus tomorrow. Let me speak with Cael.

Hi Dad.

Hi Cael. Everything okay?

Yeah.

Good.

Are you coming home?

Yeah, I'm on a bus tomorrow. I'll see ya in a few days.

Ok, good.

I miss you.

Yeah, I miss you too.

Love ya.

I love you too.

Finn closed his phone, put it in his pocket, and walked alone across the town square.

Zander and Lizzy walk on, upon a path known only to the man before them. And why were they? Walking in these woods alone with a man like that and not a single friend there to walk with them even though these woods were the same woods—and where were they going? Oh yeah, California, and maybe this way was the right way, and all the days of sunny blue skies were just about upon them.

Zander put his hand to Lizzy's shoulder, his recent markings on his arm, the blood there dried and dark, bright red around the etching: 18 88 14. Let's go back.

No, we mustn't.

The Monkey King stops and looks around, for what they wonder? They look too. For all the little lost children of the woods. And these woods were silent.

His words now, coming to them as if not in need of the very air carrying them. We're almost there, it's not far, and they walk more, into the woods of forty years back from time here.

Every Sunday morning and Wednesday evenings the Harvest Wright Bible Chapel swelled with the joy and glory of who they were. Not anymore, the small, white, clapboard Baptist church with a broken steeple, filled mostly, from time-to-time, with groups of people meeting when they could, and did not mind using a side entrance of a decaying church on a quiet shaded street.

Your adversary is known by many names.

A high ceiling with exposed rafters angling toward one another and meeting in the center.

Not just the Devil.

The pews, the finest white oak.

He walks among us.

A big stage with a big Jesus.

The Tempter.

A place of worship, that was always full.

The Deceiver.

Thousands of people, from several states.

Lucifer.

White people only. Not by policy, by design.

The minister, a tall man with slicked-back black hair, a black robe over a black suit, shiny black leather shoes, paced the stage speaking into a wireless microphone, his hands pushing the air forward, and he said, Satan. He stopped on the stage facing his congregation. We must resist all thoughts meant to lead us astray, away from the path of who we are. He looked upward, his hands moving up, God's own children. The chosen ones. His true believers. He looked back at the congregation. It's our destiny, and we must—we shall, return to a life lived in His name. It's the only way. And he said, humble before God.

As one, the congregation said, praise Jesus.

Jake stepped inside and closed the door. He crossed the cluttered room and sat on an aged block of cracked white oak. I talked to Sugar.

Oh?

Grab me one of them beers, would ya?

Jared stepped out from under a jacked up '69 Firebird and grabbed two beers from the fridge. He handed one to his brother. How'd that go?

'Bout as good as you'd think. He opened his beer and threw the cap at the garbage can and tipped it back. By the way, you didn't say nothin to Alice, did ya?

Nope.

Good, I wouldn't think you would.

Why?

I dunno, probably nothin.

Jared placed his beer on the workbench and walked back under the car. He leaned down and said, so, when ya think ya'll know?

Know what?

What it is you're thinkin about.

I dunno. Jake tipped back the last of his beer and threw the empty at the garbage can. I gotta think about it some more. He stood and walked to the door. I'm late for work.

Yeah, okay, said Jared. Later.

Yeah, said Jake, later.

He drove through town lifting his hand easy from the wheel and nodding sometimes at others in their pickups, a few cars too.

Sipping his coffee, Jake pulled into the main gate of the mill and parked in the employee's lot. He walked with his coffee and lunch cooler toward a side entrance.

Sugar walked across the close-cut lawn from her house to theirs, her flip-flops smacking her heels, her white short dress tight all the way down.

She reached the gravel driveway behind Jared's house and stepped over a scattering of kid's toys and opened the drive-shed door. I suppose you know already?

Jared didn't answer and he didn't look out from under the car.

She walked to the fridge and grabbed a beer and opened it and took a sip. She walked around the car and sat on the high stool at the workbench. She crossed her legs, her one leg bouncing, her flip-flop staying on her foot by some force of unseen logic. Well, whatever, and she took another sip.

Jared stepped out from under the car and grabbed a rag from the workbench and turned and leaned against the bench and wiped his hands. He took the beer from her and took a sip. What'd he say?

She got up and walked to the fridge and grabbed another beer. She closed the fridge door and looked at the calendar hanging on the wall, some girl with less than little on draped over the hood of a shiny red car. They make good money, ya know. She opened the beer and looked back at the poster. A blonde, like her. It's not just the money, it's the connections. She looked back at Jared. Ya know that, right?

He watched her duck under the car and walk hunched over under it.

She pulled herself onto the stool and crossed her legs and took a sip.

Well?

He just said, I'm shootin blanks. Like I didn't know that already.

Jared walked back under the car. He didn't say nothin else?

Nope. She took a sip of beer and hung her wrist with the beer in her hand over the knee of her bouncing leg. Why? He say somethin to you, or somethin?

Nope. Just that he had to think about it some more.

Oh, he's good at that, all right. Thinkin all the time and never sayin nothin. Say, ya miss it down there?

Where?

The mill, where else?

Nope, not a single weepin moment. Not one. Why?

It wasn't much of a settlement though, was it? Least that's what Jake says. And you can hardly tell at all with your leg now.

The Spaldings aren't in the habit of givin up much, that's for damn sure.

No, I guess that's right. He never talks about it, ya know.

What's that?

Her.

Who?

Amanda Spalding.

Oh, her. No, I guess he doesn't.

I thought he was a real somebody, ya know, back then.

What'ya sayin, ya don't think he is now?

Oh, I suppose he is, in his own way, I guess.

Yeah, well, when he got hurt and couldn't play collage, he—
I don't know, changed, I guess, at least for a while. Like he was
just going through the motions.

He won't settle for this, you know.

Jared bent down and looked at Sugar. Settle for what?

Not havin kids.

I guess there's not much he can do about it, is there?

She took a sip of beer and switched up her legs, dropping
her wrist over her knee. I have not a single idea about that. Not
when it comes to him, I don't. I saw Alice get in late last night.
Why's that?

They got inventory down there.

Oh? How long she been there anyway? It's been awhile, ain't
it?

He walked back to the bench and picked up his beer and
took a sip. Where? The Piggly Wiggly?

Un-huh. Where else?

I suppose she has, why?

No reason. I just can't see anybody wantin to stay there all
that long, that's all.

She likes it well enough. He set his beer back down and turned and stood in front of Sugar, his hands reaching past her to the workbench.

She uncrossed her legs and leaned back resting on her elbows. We need to get the hell out of here.

I'm working on it.

Well, work harder, cause we gotta go. There's nothin good comin from any of this. I just know it. I can feel it.

We will. Not long now, and he pulled her to him, her legs wrapping around him.

You Burleson's are all the same.

Is that right, he said. We'll see about that, won't we? and he kissed her, pulling her to him harder.

In that big house, atop of that high hill, Sterling Spalding sat alone in a dark room without windows. Two big chandeliers reflecting a dim light sparkling down the will of his control.

He ran the trains, and he ran them over long Parker truss bridges, through towns, around bends, and over green fields. He ran them through the station, past the people, and high over the hills too.

Look at em go. Shiny and go. Round and round.

He put the box down, his big cigar between his big fingers and he dimmed the lights more. He sat back in his big chair and watched the trains go. Slow and steady. Slow and steady now. His heavy crystal glass in his hand and he put it all back. He blew more big smoke over the big train world. The trains moving on. He poured more whiskey and he smoked more. He moved forward more. His dark eyes in a dark world watching the trains go. A slow train coming. Save our cities—we tried that, did we not? With far too much time and money, but no longer. Never again. Save our souls—no. Those days are done and gone, and we will not allow ourselves to be held hostage by the bankrupt morals of the many. Never again. Same sex marriage? You want a war, you got one—it's coming. This future of ours, certain, by the very word of our one true lord.

One nation within a nation.

The trains moving on. Look at em go. Shiny and go. Round and round.

He drank more and he smoked more. He took the big cigar from his mouth and he reached forward and jabbed the air, that burn, that sting. He jabbed again. He jabbed harder. We shall not be denied. Louder in the dark. Never, and not in this, the time of us now.

Never fucking again.

Quiet in the dark, the trains moving on, and like the spoken keys of a refrain, he said, humble before God. Praise Jesus.

And this man, one of the last kings, stood in the dark, a light he had dimmed himself, and he stepped forward and shut the trains down, and the silence that came was like a rattle and hum, like the piled and broken bones of all of us against the coming winds of our certainties. Of knowing itself. For we must secure the existence of our people and a future for our children. Must we not?

He got up and walked out of the room and closed the door behind him, the trains runnin on.

Look at em go. Shiny and go. Round and round.

PART THREE

There was a bench in front of the store, and in the shade of the heat he was there, little, his feet swinging over the faded sidewalk boards, watching his grandfather oil up his work boots.

His grandfather looked up at the man standing before him. Everett.

It's comin off some, said Everett.

Seems like it.

Cael watched Everett strike a wooden match, light a cigarette and blow out the match. He watched him flip the match around and put the good end of it in his ear and work it around in there.

What'ya have in store for those?

I'm takin the boy here fishin.

Sunday morning?

Yes sir, Sunday morning.

Cael looked to the street and saw that girl walking with her mother. She looked too. She smiled. Cael smiled back. On her way to church, he thought.

We won't be seein you in chapel then? said Everett.

Oh, ya'll be seein me all right, the same way ya see me every Sunday morning. He looked at Cael, and Cael looked at his grandfather, and together they said, on the river.

Cael looked back at the girl, still walking away with her mother down the empty main street.

His grandfather looked too. She's a pretty girl.

Cael looked away, at his grandfather's oiled work boot on the bench next to him. He looked at his own shoes. He didn't know about work boots, but he liked fishing.

A big diesel Three-Fifty pulled up. The engine turned off and a man stepped out wearing wide black leather shoes, the thin black laces undone. He was a fat man, with heavy red cheeks, a wide sagging neck, his thin white short-sleeved shirt pulled tight around his big belly, straining the buttons. He had a buzz cut with a flattop. He hiked his pants up and Cael looked at the beads of sweat on the man's forehead.

It's hotter than the front porch of Hades.

Maybe ya ain't standing on the porch no more, Hector?

Oh, I'm all right, Everett. Using a handkerchief he held in his hand, he wiped the sweat from his forehead. I ain't seen you yet? He leaned into the truck, the back of his shirt dark with sweat and stuck to him. He came out holding some motor for something. An appliance maybe. Sheldon, what the hell is this thing missing? He stepped onto the faded splintered sidewalk boards and passed the motor to Cael's grandfather.

Sheldon put his boot down fend put up his glasses and looked at the motor. He looked over his glasses at Hector. You're missing a gasket.

Everett chuckled.

Ya got one?

Should do. Mackenzie?

She came to the door, her phone in her hand.

Do you know where we keep the appliance motor gaskets?

She shook her head, no.

Come with me, Hector.

I'm all right here. You go on and I'll keep an eye on Finn's young boy here and make sure he walks a straight line. Lord knows, I never could with his father.

You're not the sheriff anymore, Hector, what he does, or doesn't do, is none of your damn business. He walked into the store and Cael looked down the sidewalk at a tall woman with a big floppy hat, a long summer dress and sandals walking with a small boy wearing a blue polo shirt, neat khakis shorts, and little white running shoes with white socks.

A balding man wearing a bright flowered Hawaiian shirt, shorts and running shoes with black socks, walked by the other way. He was wearing aviator sunglasses and puffing on a cigarette held in a long black holder.

No one spoke.

Cael turned and saw a red kite, untethered, drifting in the high warm air against the flat blue sky.

Sheldon returned with the motor part. There you go, mayor, two-fifty.

The mayor reached into his pocket and took out a five-dollar bill and handed it to Sheldon. Never mind the change, give it to the boy there and let em get an ice cream. Boys. He walked back to his truck and got in and drove away.

Go on then, Cael, get Mackenzie, and go and get that ice cream.

Jake lowered the sports section of the morning paper and looked at Amanda Spalding taking off her hat, repositioning her long hair down her back. He looked at the young boy standing next to her.

Amanda looked at her son. She looked at Jake. Well now, Jake Burleson.

Jake stood. He looked again at the boy. And who's this?

This is Hunter. She put her hand to the boy's head. Sweetie, can you say hello to Mr. Burelson?

Jake bent down and offered his hand. Jake.

The little boy shook the tips of Jake's fingers.

It's nice to meet you, Hunter. Are ya here for an ice cream?

The boy let go of Jake's fingers.

What flavor?

He likes strawberry. Don't you, Hunter?

Hunter nodded.

Strawberry's good, but not as good as chocolate, and he looked at Amanda and held up two fingers. Two scoops. He winked at Cael and Mackenzie standing waiting behind them. Cael smiled and Mackenzie did not.

Finn woke and walked across the vacant town square. He stopped and looked around. He looked at the sky. It was lower yet, and he walked again. Where? He needed a room for the night, focus on that, he thought. And he did, and he walked more yet.

A light summer dress on, barefoot, she steps from the porch and she walks across the short dead grass, stepping around discarded items of some past wanting. She stops at a little wooden gate with chipped white paint, and she looks at the shaded woods and the stream where she does not like to go.

Lizzy. Zander.

She crosses her arms as if she were cold in that dead flat heat.

Lizzy.

Her hands digging into her arms, squeezing.

Zander.

Not even a breeze to welcome her words.

Lizzy. Zander.

Just the names of her two children, missing.

Where are you? And why won't you come home?

Standing at the stove cooking off cocaine, the man turns and looks out the screen door, and in the coming dark he can hear his wife again: Lizzy. Zander.

In that place, these many years later, the sound of the children's mother's voice, there still, and echoing: Lizzy. Zander. Why won't you come home?

His camp is at the crux of where a shallow stream cuts away from the Tidewater River, a wide hard-packed shoreline of smooth stones and sand. At the edge of the trees there's a shelter made of branches open to the southeast, filled with leaves and pine needles and covered in the skin of a black bear.

A hare cooks upright on two green willow branches.

He reaches to the edges of the coals and picks out a mud-packed ear of corn and Zander squints at the imagined pain of the hot coals.

They watch him blow dry baked mud embedded with orange embers away from the burnt husks of corn.

They eat their meal, not speaking, the sun falling.

Born of this world, the Monkey King says, and yet, is the world itself.

The hare? asks Lizzy.

Yes. Do you suppose it liked being a hare?

Yes, I think so, says Lizzy. He was a nice hare.

Yes, I think so too. But its knowing it was a hare, or not a hare, did not change it from being this hare. He looks at the children, and they are silent, and he leans back, and he laughs, his bigger than all-the-world laugh. We need music, he says, and he plays on, the fire burning on, his eyes holding them, looking, and looking beyond them, this man, the Monkey King man, playing his harp for all the little lost children, the fire burning higher, twists of gray smoke and orange embers pushing up his notes, a warm southern breeze taking them away.

To where?

Their mother? Time coming? To Finn, all alone, and remembering?

And remembering still.

He lowers his harp, the last of his notes lingering, now, as if calling to us, and waiting, and he says, the more you get to the end of everything, the end of your faith, your beliefs, your certainties, the very end of knowing itself, it's what's there and waiting.

What? asks Zander.

The beginning, of course.

Lizzy smiles, and the Monkey King smiles too.

He puts the children to bed and covers them in the heaviness of the bearskin. He sits and watches Zander sleeping, but not Lizzy, her eyes wide, out-waiting the pain in the night, in the coming dark, and he puts his hand to her forehead—there there now—now now, and she squeezes her fists, and she closes her eyes, and she flees again, a little girl on the back of duskywings.

Never again, my dear, Lizzy. Never again.

He folded and packed away his clothes and walked out of the laundromat and down the sidewalk, past the stores and cafes, and he came to a side street. He stopped and looked. There was a small hotel with a shaded sign coming out from the wall above the door, The Black Swan.

A man stood by the door waiting, some happily misplaced person, or so it seemed to him, as if from another place and time, his white-gloved hand reaching for the long brass door handle. Allow me, sir.

It's not sir, it's just Finn.

My dad used to tell me, never say 'just' when speaking of yourself, or what it is you do.

I'll remember that, thanks. And Finn stuck his hand out.

The man said, Booker, and shook Finn's hand.

Is it a good place?

It was once the choice of kings.

Is that right. And now?

Times are hard, sir—Finn. He pulled the door open. Enjoy your stay.

Thanks, Booker. Finn stopped. What about a steak? Nothing too elaborate, a diner maybe?

The Sunday Morning Café does up a good one.

Thanks.

The man smiled and nodded and Finn walked inside.

He walked across the faded red carpet with a worn gold design of some sort and up to the front desk. There was a woman there, a young one.

Welcome to the Black Swan.

I need a room for the night.

One night?

Yes, please, one, with a window that opens, if ya got it, at the back.

One minute, sir—.

Finn.

Here we go. I have just the one. She looked up. Room 509.

It's at the back?

Yes, it is.

Great.

Sign here. We'll need a credit card.

I have cash.

Cash?

Yes.

One moment. She walked through a paneled door next to a bank of wooden mail holders.

Finn waited. He turned and looked at the portraits of old white men hanging on the textured wallpaper.

The hotel requires a two hundred dollar deposit.

How much is the room?

Eighty-five.

He reached into his pocket and pulled out a roll of money and counted out the bills and placed them on the counter.

She put the money in a cash drawer.

He signed in and she handed him the key. Do you require another key? Is there a Mrs.—she looked at the sign-in card—Finley?

Nope.

If there's anything I can do, anything at all, please just let me know.

I will, thanks.

She brushed her hair with long slow strokes and looked out the French doors, the white linen curtains blowing over the dark marbled floor, the sweet scent of a distant breeze reaching her with its wanting, and taking, these scents of yesterday. Days gone by. Days not wanted here. And yet, days that will not take their leave, or so it seemed.

Hunter in his pajamas, fresh and clean, behind her, playing with a toy train engine on the floor.

Marisa came in and Amanda looked back. I'll be right there. She looked again to that place beneath the moonlight, the length of one more brush stroke all the time she needed to not ask why.

To not need to.

Jake took a sip of beer and drove slow through the town not going anywhere, not really. At the lights he stopped and he sipped his beer and rolled on washed in green and he nodded at the driver of a passing pickup truck.

Finn opened the window to try and free from the small room the old smell coming from the walls and the few pieces of worn furniture. He looked out the window at an overgrown garden walled by a high black wrought iron fence covered in creeping ivy. An older couple, sitting on a bench with a small table in front of them, looked up and smiled, and he did too.

He pulled back the bedspread and folded it and slid it under the bed. He turned down the white sheet and put his bag up. He unzipped it and took out a clean shirt and a pair of jeans. He sat on the bed and took his boots off listening to the couple's quiet voices lifting up to him by the stillness of that place. A stillness he was unsure of. He looked at the painting on the wall across from him. Like that, he thought. Keep it all together, just like that. The faint hum of a dawn's mist rising over the quietness of waterlilies in the distance. He tucked his boots part way under the bed and walked to the bathroom and took a hot shower, just standing there, leaning his hands against the wall, the months falling away, the mountains, the high slash, the burn—all of it. And he said, Lizzy.

He's there still, siting in the dark watching over them, Lizzy's tears tried and fallen, the rattling of her hollowing, fear chewing bones and soft tissue, all coming to him and settling heavy upon him.

Lizzy's eyes opening, looking off somewhere else.

It's me, Lizzy, says the Monkey King. We've known each other a long time. A real long time. We're friends.

She looks at him, pausing, studying him, her eyes widening—Buster, and she folds herself into the good covering of him. His heart. His bones. Her tears coming.

My dear little, Lizzy.

You came for me.

Of course, I did. I've never not been here. You know that. Time stretches all the way back to when we were the very same, and then before even that, and again before that—a continuum. Of course, it is, and you can remember that, too, if ya wanted to.

Zander awake now, in the dark, and whoever knows what is out there, waiting? And he says, what'ya mean we were the same?

The man looks at Zander. The very same.

That's not true.

Oh, but it is, Zander. It's as true as the very touch of me.

What color?

That original man and me, the one and the very same.

That's a lie, and you know it.

Leaning closer to Zander, the Monkey King's eyes widen, the whites of them upon him, and he puts his hand to Zander's face, Zander squinting at the touch. At the hum that comes. We were, Zander, at one time, the very same, despite what you might think, or think it ought to be, or what you've been told. He looks at Zander's forearm, at the red-rimmed recent markings.

Lizzy looks too. He didn't do that.

Zander moves his arm away and sits up. If that's true, why aren't we the same still?

Geography and a nomadic curiosity, I suppose. That and a happy ever-loving on-going resilience. Our bodies are such wonderful things, and capable of such great change. And he looks to the dark and what he sees there. Like the earth itself.

He puts his hand to Zander's recent tattoo, the one forced upon him. Can you feel that, Zander? For it is there, all of our time, requiring only that you look, and in doing so, seeing you. For this time of ours, it was shared time, and always will be. He looks to the river, at the moon reflecting upon a low rippling section. What do you say we cool down?

Amanda stops, on the downslope of the grassy hill, beneath the moonlight. This is private property.

Jake didn't look back, the town before him, the mighty river. This whole goddamn town is private property, he says, and he looks back at Amanda, in her nightgown, standing above him. What about it?

She leaned against a tall pine tree and looked at Jake sitting on the crest of the hill looking back at her. She crossed her arms in front of her and she looked past him to the Tidewater sky.

He looked at her nightgown moving in the night breeze.

It's still so beautiful, though, isn't it?

He looked back at the town. I guess, but don't let that fool ya.

She edged her way down the slope and sat next to him.

He opened a beer and handed it to her.

So, Sugar? How's that?

I dunno.

She took a sip of beer. You can do better than that, Jake. How long's it been?

He looked at Amanda. A while now.

Kids?

Nope. Tell me about Hunter. He seems like a nice kid.

He is, thanks. There's not much to tell. His father's an artist, a good one. He's very talented. Jean-Baptiste Duval.

You're just home visiting then? I heard different.

Did you?

Yup, but you know how that goes.

Yes, I do, and I haven't missed it. Not in the slightest.

They sat looking at the town, the roofs of the small houses, the river, and farther down, the mill, and the big hazy moon of that night, hanging over everything.

I wanted Hunter to see this.

I can understand that.

She looked at Jake. I wondered if you were still here.

Well, here I am. A lifer, it seems. Sad enough, I suppose, huh?

I wouldn't say that, no.

I wrote you.

Let's not talk about it.

I could have come.

She looked at Jake. It was such a horrible time. First my mother, and then my brother. She took his arm in hers and leaned her head on his shoulder. Let's just sit for a while and not talk, and they do, time holding them in the night beneath the moon and they wonder, will it always?

Wrapped in a towel he walked across the room and sat on the bed and stretched out leaning his head against the pillow.

He was restless and he sat up.

He stood and he walked to the window. He opened it more and lit a cigarette and looked down at the courtyard, the old couple no longer there.

He thought of his son, Cael. You were up and out of the car so fast.

I forgot.

I took the stairs two-at-a-time and you were there, with such a look on your face. He exhaled a stream of smoke and thought to himself, do not ever forget that look.

You said to me, there's blood in there.

He flicked the cigarette out the window and walked to the bathroom and opened a beer and walked to the armchair and sat down.

He closed their bedroom door. There was so much blood, everywhere.

He took a sip.

I wanted to tell you, it's okay, but you were already walking back down the stairs.

I had given you your pill, Lizzy. Why'd you wake up? You shouldn't have. Where was it all coming from, he had thought— there, and I pulled back the blankets—there, and more yet, there.

All those pills, each one, each time, the last time.

Do I take you, or do I call? I had put the kids in a room and told them, it's okay.

Don't promise.

He realized he was standing back at the window looking down at the empty square.

I took the curtains down and cleaned and bandaged you. I took the sheets off the bed. They'll come when I'm gone.

He looked back at the room he was standing in, old and tired with just enough space to live.

Do you want me to call someone?

No, the kids had said to him, just go.

Cael?

He didn't look. C'mon, Cael, look at me.

He looked again at the room he was in, as if to try and orientate himself. The dresser. The polished floor. Who was it that had been here before him, he thought. What were they like? What did they know? What had happened to them?

What did they need?

Cael still wouldn't look.

He told them, it'll be all right, I promise. I'll close the door and you can come out when you hear me go.

I walked back up the stairs and put you on my shoulder, Lizzy, and walked back down the stairs and out the door.

I put you in the backseat of the car, got in, and just sat there, in the dark.

And I wondered.

He sipped his beer.

Who was coming to help?

No one, he said out loud, and he took another sip of beer.

And he was wondering that still.

The cool clear midnight water runs over them.

Close your eyes and stretch your arms behind you. Do not be afraid. Let go. Let it take you.

And they do.

Can you feel it?

They smile and he smiles, his gold tooth reflecting the moonlight, and they're quiet, only the sounds of the water running over them, the good feel of it, the endlessness of time within it.

Everything we know, or think we know, is going. It's changing. Like the rocks beneath us. Our ability to do so is our strength and our freedom. And we must embrace it and never turn our backs to it.

Lizzy closes her eyes and thinks, she's never gonna move away from this spot, right here.

Never.

And Zander asks, does everything always change?

Yes, says the Monkey King. If north can become south, and south can become north, what can't change?

That can happen?

Did happen.

It did?

Yup. Forty-two thousand years ago.

That's a long time, says Zander.

Yes, it is, says the Monkey King, but fortunately, it was only for the blink of an eye. A mere few hundred years or so. But let us enjoy this now; this place; this time here, these beautiful waters flowing over us, the echoing within it. Under that one same moon.

Echoing? asks Zander.

Yes, says the Monkey King. Listen. Can you hear it? It's all there for you. Everything. It always has been.

Lizzy, with her eyes still closed, smiles, and she whispers, yes, I can hear it.

Rain slashing in the open door darkened the concrete floor. Jake closed the door. He walked to the fridge and grabbed a beer. I need to talk to ya.

Jared grabbed a rag from the workbench.

Remember when I said I had to figure out what to do. You know, about what the doc said?

Yeah.

Well, I think I got it.

Oh?

It might sound a little crazy, at least, at first it might, but when you really think about it, it ain't that crazy. He took a sip of beer. You know how much Sugar wants kids.

Right.

Not that I don't, cause I do. I mean, you got your two and they're doin okay, right?

I guess. I mean, it seems like it.

The thing is, I don't wanna adopt some stranger's baby and say it's mine. Sugar don't neither. We could get her artificially knocked up, but we can't afford it. Anyway, we wouldn't want to.

And?

And, that leaves just one thing.

It does?

Yup.

What?

I want you to do it.

You what?

You heard me.

What the fuck, Jake. Are you asking me to fuck Sugar?

Yup.

Does Sugar know about this?

We talked about it.

You talked about it?

Yup.

What about Alice? Ya think she's gonna be all right with me walking next door and havin a go with Sugar? Cause I got news for ya, she won't be.

She doesn't gotta know.

What'ya mean she doesn't gotta know? How the hell is she ain't gonna know?

Cause we ain't gonna tell her, that's how.

For fuck's sake, Jake. This is nuts. I can't fuck Sugar.

What'ya mean you can't fuck Sugar? She looks good still.

Well, yeah, she does, but—.

So?

C'mon, Jake, get serious. I can't fuck her.

I'm as serious as the day is long, little brother. Hell, it won't take more than a time-or-two—didn't ya always tell me all ya had to do to get Alice pregnant was to hang your pants on the bedpost? Think about it. At least the kid'll be a Burelson. Besides, you don't gotta worry about a thing, I got it all worked out. He took a last sip of his beer and threw the empty at the garbage can. Don't say nothin now, just think about it. He walked to the door, stopped and looked back. Oh, by-the-way, Sugar says she'll be dropping eggs in the next day or so.

She'll be what?

Yup, that's what she said. Later, said Jake, and he walked out the door.

Yeah, later, said Jared. Fuck me.

PART FOUR

In her long silk nightgown, Amanda walked barefoot the polished marble floors of the dark house. Hunter sleeping. Her father too. Like a ghost, she thought. Moving through this house. A ghost of a ghost.

Might as well be, like all the others.

She tried the train room door. It wasn't locked and she opened it. It was dark and it was quiet and she didn't turn the light on.

It disturbed her still, images of herself as a little girl on her father's knee. The smell of his cigars and whiskey. His eyes so fierce in their intent.

I could've been anyone.

People's beliefs—family's beliefs, even worse, she thought. Nothing is more unsightly. More disturbing. These convictions of belief, and always there. Our memories, too, twisting and turning, these frozen moments of time held on to.

Why give room to someone not deserving of the space we hold for them?

These needs of us.

Well, fuck that, she thought.

So much of it always just like that. The trick of light in a room with the door closed, and she walked more the open spaces of the big house, looking at all the closed doors and not caring, or even thinking about, what might be behind them.

There were rooms she did like. The Conservatory. She opened the French doors. All the scents and colors. The warmth. The moisture in the air. She touched the plants as she walked, her mother coming to her mind, bent over, kneeling, looking back at her, smiling, saying, come in, dear. Close the door and come and help me.

The purity of her honest intent. The goodness of it.

Come in and help me.

She stood there for a long time. Mum, she said. Mum, and there were tears in her eyes.

Look, he has a gun, says Lizzy.

Yes, says the Monkey King.

Zander asks, who are they?

A shotgun over his shoulder, walking slow and easy on a rutted truck path through the quiet heavy woods following a light blue and white Bronco. A Black man with a gun and not a worry in the world.

Not one.

Agitators.

Agitators? asks Lizzy.

The truck comes to a clearing filled with old pickups, a flatbed truck, and a few cars. There were vehicle doors open with legs hanging out, others sleeping in the back of pickups and on the ground.

On the back of the flatbed truck was a long, thin, naked redheaded white woman, draped over the body of a naked Black man.

A large bonfire pit in the center of the clearing, long twists of ashy gray smoke.

Doing things to upset others.

Why? asks Lizzy.

For money.

The Bronco stops and a man steps out.

Oh, he's tall and he has no hair, says Lizzy.

Zander leans closer, trying to see the man better. He looks at the Monkey King. He looks back at the man. Are they goin to Tidewater?

No, Zander, somewhere else.

The man closes the door of the Bronco. An older man, tall and bald with a thick mustache, gold, round, wire-rimmed glasses, and heavy, black work boots, jeans, a collared shirt with an open vest, and a big silver watch on his left wrist.

His name is Zachary.

Zander looks at Lizzy. He looks back at the man. The very same man, and he remembers: It was all packed away in an old brown satchel case and they were wanting to blow another bowel. The music too loud and the Englishman growing impatient.

Standing at his partially opened bedroom door, Zander remembers looking back at Lizzy sleeping in her bed. When he looked back, the man was looking at him, smiling, a big smile showing his large and unsightly teeth. It had scared Zander, and he had closed his bedroom door and gone back to bed.

Just one more, he had heard his mother say. Just one.

No, I'm good, and he heard the man leaving, the screen door slapping shut behind him.

In his bed, Zander's hands had moved up, one after the other, over and over. Over and over climbing. You can do it, sweet baby boy, and he climbed more, the feeling of everything from that house running through him electric. This acquiring of their fears. Their beliefs. Climb harder, baby boy. Climb harder yet. You'll get there, and he knew he would, but before he did, he told himself, he'd kill him.

Not the man before him now.

His father.

Kill em dead.

Desperate to understand anything good, Zander had climbed on into the night, like most nights, over and over, and up and up. The heat, his hatred of that place, his father, all pulsing through his veins, pushing him on. The light of the moon not breaking through to him.

Not yet.

Not now.

Maybe not ever.

At the Bronco parked in their driveway, the man had looked toward the top of the driveway, at another car parked there, dark and not running.

He pulled up to the car and stopped.

Hector waiting. Everything okay?

The Englishman nodded and drove on.

And now there were tears in Zander's eyes.

The Monkey King looking.

Lizzy too.

Is everything okay, Zander? the Monkey King asks.

Zander clears the tears from his eyes, and says, why wouldn't it be? He looks at Lizzy. We're never goin home again, Lizzy. Never. No matter what. He looks at the Monkey King. And don't think we are, cause we're not. And you can't make us.

No, that's right, Zander. We're goin to California.

Yes, says Zander. California.

Yes, says Lizzy. California.

Amanda came out from the arched hallway to the main entrance and looked at the big winding staircase. She walked to the back of it and stepped forward more and looked closer.

He wasn't worth it.

Not nearly, was he worth it.

Why?

Why here?

Why then?

The image in her mind of her brother, swaying gently by a rope he'd placed around his neck.

She turned away and walked to the front doors and opened them, standing looking out past the manicured lawns and gardens, the fountain, the long circular driveway that was not lined now with cars as it was so many times before, each time marking the days of her youth, one celebration after another, money spilling over the moments defining her little-girl-happiness.

A warm night breeze picking up and pushing over her.

It chilled her.

The ghost of that little girl. And all the other ones there with her now, she thought.

Waiting and wanting.

For what she wondered?

The making of monsters. Intentional, or otherwise. But always, monsters, all the very same.

And she cried more. Tears of her remembering. Her younger self there with her, with tears in her eyes too. She was sure of it. How could there not be?

The sheriff 's here.

Go on and talk to him. I'll be out in a minute.

She steps onto the porch, the squeak of the boards, the screen door slapping shut, the evening heat coming to her, and she watches the sheriff get out and walk around the car and lean against the front of it.

Kerry.

Sheriff.

Where's Edward at?

She looks back at the house.

We checked at the school. Nobody's seen em.

No?

Alice said they never got on the bus.

Buttoning his shirt up, Edward walks out the door. Sheriff.

She looks back at her husband. They never got on the bus.

We checked with Alice, says the sheriff.

They'll be hearing about this, that's for damn sure.

Any problems lately? Last night, say?

Nope, none. He looks at his wife.

She looks away from her husband, and looks back at the sheriff. Nothin like that, no.

The sheriff looks behind him, at the woods. What about in there?

We checked. Nothin, says Edward.

She looks to the woods and crosses her arms and she thinks, Lizzy, Zander.

The sheriff pushes off the car, we'll talk to folks in town in case they show up there. In the meantime, if you think of anything, or they show back here, let us know.

He gets in the car, backs it up, and pulls away.

She looks at her husband, leaning past the broken porch railing and spitting to the dry dirt.

What the fuck are you lookin at?

She watches him walk into the house and she turns and looks back to the woods, her hand coming to the back of her neck.

Later, not knowing how long she'd been standing there, the porch boards still warm beneath her bare feet, her dress sticking to her, she whispers, Lizzy. Zander.

She knows that's where they are, and why, alone in the woods like that, like she once was.

Please, come home. We could leave and I could get better. I know I can.

Please God, let me try.

Again.

One more time again.

Please.

But, of course, no one hears her. Not here now, not back then, when she was just little herself and lost in those very same woods.

Buster. Bring them home, please.

She wipes the tears from her eyes. Buster?

Someone, please.

And in the warm night air of her remembering, she cries more.

They watched a young girl, they couldn't remember her name, and her much larger, older brother, the one with a mental impairment, walking along a fence, poking sticks into the tall grass, grasshoppers popping up everywhere.

They heard the large overgrown man-boy say, I dropped it here somewhere.

Mackenzie slapped Cael on the arm and said, don't stare.

I wasn't.

Yes, you were, liar.

Never mind, I don't lie.

Then don't.

Let's get home for dinner, Cael said.

It's too hot to eat, said Mackenzie.

She'll be wondering.

Don't ya wanna just stay here in the shade and keep your feet in the water?

I can do it anytime. I'm hungry now.

You're always hungry.

I know it, but she cooks good.

You're as dumb as Benny over there.

Cael looked. Maybe he's not dumb?

Maybe.

C'mon, said Cael, we gotta go.

You go on, tell em I'm at the library.

All right, but don't be too long. He'll come lookin.

He walked into the diner and sat at the counter.

A waitress walked up, an older woman.

Coffee, please.

She left to get his coffee and Finn looked around at the few people there, a young couple at a center table, three older men drinking coffee and talking at a back table, another man sitting on his own, a woman sitting at a front window table, thin, with short reddish hair, beautiful green eyes, a nose ring.

The waitress brought his coffee.

He looked at the waitress, looking at her scratch pad, her pencil ready. I'll take a steak, he said. Medium rare with fries.

Anything else?

A Red Cap.

Ain't got it.

Budweiser's fine.

He sipped his coffee and looked again at the woman by the window.

She stood and walked to the door and looked back at Finn, her eyes holding a sadness, somewhat like a conviction, that fate was here now. She could feel it. Not in the past. Not tomorrow. Now. And fate, she knew, always won. She opened the door and walked outside.

A young girl, with long flowing hair, stood on the sidewalk boards watching the woman walking away. She turned and looked in the café window, and she saw Finn, who turned and looked at her.

In the pre-dawn dark, Jake and Jared passed one another crossing their adjoining lots. They nodded at one another.

Jake opened the tin-shed door and switched the light on and walked to the fridge and grabbed a beer and walked to the workbench and dragged a stool to the window facing his place and he leaned to his side and turned the light back off and he sat drinking his beer looking out to the dark.

Alice at the kitchen window. Without expression. Watching the light at Jake and Sugar's house turn off.

It's in the here and now, tomorrow comes, thought Jake. Not the past. And what a day that will be.

What a fuckin day that will be, indeed.

What a fuckin day is right, said Jake.

The Quiet Man drove north on the interstate.

In the boardroom at the head office of the mill Sterling was on his phone. There were fifteen or sixteen other men in suits watching him. He flipped his phone shut, and he said, they passed it.

An older man with short well-brushed white hair looked at Sterling and said, humble before God.

Sterling and the other men said, yes, praise Jesus.

Amanda walked the gardens of Sterling estate with Hunter. She stopped and looked at the town below her, at Jake's house. Sugar, she thought, and she smiled, of all the girls in this town, of course, it had to be you.

She looked back at the house. At the wide stone steps leading to the house. Holding Hunter's hand, she walked up the steps. She walked to the side of the house and picked up a trail through the high manicured gardens and she came to a clearing. Her studio. Or, at least, it once was. A dark board and baton building with a high black tin roof, large black and glass lanterns on either side of wide wooden doors.

It was unlocked, and she walked inside. She turned a light on.

A large chandelier hung from the center of the ceiling over a large workspace counter. A sitting area to the right with several chairs and a couch, a television mounted over a stone and glass fireplace. A bar with a kitchen area. There were paintings on the walls, and more of them stacked in rows to the back right. To the left, a large work-in-progress iron sculpture, at least twelve feet in height. There was a portable staircase pushed up to it. It was of a mother, leaning back, twirling her young daughter by her hands, the girl's hair flying behind her, her dress ruffling. To the back left, other sculptures. Some finished, others not, all different shapes and sizes and done in different mediums.

What's that? asked Hunter.

Something Mommy made.

When?

A long time ago.

It's big.

Yes, it is.

Who is it?

A mother and her daughter.

What's the girl's name?

Sunday, said Amanda.

Like the ice cream, said Hunter.

No, Hunter, like the day of the week. C'mon, we should go, and she turned the lights off—to that time, and she closed the door behind them.

They're riding easy on his shoulders. So what's in California?

Our uncle lives there, says Lizzy.

He does? On whose side?

Our mother's brother, says Zander.

Uncle William, says Lizzy.

Where in California does he live?

Neither one speaks, and they look at one another.

California is big you know.

It is? says Lizzy.

Oh, yes, very big. What's your momma's last name?

Overland, just like us, says Lizzy.

Un-huh. But isn't your momma married to your daddie?

Yes, of course she is, says Lizzy.

But your uncle's not. What was your momma's name before she got married?

It wasn't Overland? says Lizzy.

Zander?

He doesn't answer.

That's okay, we're looking for Uncle William in California, and they walk on, in the woods, on their way to the sunny, forever-blue-skies of California.

Finn walked out the café door and stood on the sidewalk. He looked around. He walked the perimeter of the town square, past the shops, most of them closed, and he thought about the woman from the café. He looked at the bench in the center of the town square. No, he thought. He didn't want to get lost in his thinking. Not now. The endless remembering. He needed to keep moving, and he walked on.

To what?

He didn't know.

Not that. Not anymore.

The constant remembering, and not forgetting.

Why don't we stop here, it's a nice spot, and the Monkey King sets the kids down on a dry grassy section next to the river.

On their backs with their hands behind their heads looking up to the long, flat sky, the sun high and coming to them through blinds of thin yellow-green willow leaves twisting in the light.

The Monkey King looks at Zander's arm. Can I see that?

Zander moves his arm away.

Zander, says Lizzy, show him.

Zander looks at the Monkey King, and he holds his arm out to him, his tattoo, bright red with puss leaking from it.

It doesn't look so good. Lizzy, bring us some water.

In what?

Your hands will do.

She walks to the river's edge and she bends down and cups her hands to the running water.

When she gets back, there's only a small amount of water left in her little hands.

Right there.

She lets the water fall from her hands over Zander's forearm.

The Monkey King takes a small leather pouch from his belt and opens it. He dips his finger into it and spreads a clear minty ointment over the wound.

What's that, asks Lizzy?

It's infected. This'll help. He looks at Zander. Do you know what it means?

Zander looks at the Monkey King. I know what it means.

He didn't do it, says Lizzy.

I wouldn't imagine so, Lizzy, says the Monkey King. We'll have to keep an eye on it, but I think it'll be fine. He stands and looks up toward the sun. He looks at the children, and he scoops them up in his opened hands stretching his arms above him, twisting the children, their arms rigid and straight out before them. Their legs too. All the way to the sun, he says, and he begins to run.

The children smile and scream, looking at one another, and flying now.

We're getting closer, can you feel the heat of that perfect star? And now you're beginning to change, he runs faster, your skin is getting darker, back to the way it once was, and let's just hope we don't all burn up. He throws them up into the air and they scream. He catches them. We had better turn around, and he does, running hard again, away from the sun.

Faster faster, Lizzy screams, I'm burning up.

And now, all the way to the moon and back. Just us and no one else. For it is a light you can only know, and share, in love. And only ever that. Can you remember?

Yes, says Lizzy. Only ever with love.

Yes, he says. Love under a big moon.

Always.

Jake opened the door and walked to the fridge and opened a beer. How did it go?

Jared, standing at his workbench, didn't turn around.

Ya got it done, right?

Yeah. He looked back. But I had to turn her around.

What? Why? She looks good still.

No, I mean, to do it, ya know.

I guess. He took a sip of beer.

Maybe cause she's your wife, or somethin like that, what'ya think?

How long ya been married?

Eleven years. Why?

Do ya still love her?

What? Yeah, I guess. How the hell should I know?

It's hard to know, ain't it?

Yeah, it's not easy.

Ya think she still loves you?

Of course, she does. Why wouldn't she?

I didn't say she didn't. What about Sugar?

What about her?

Think she still loves me?

Hell, Jake, I don't know, I suppose so. Why?

I don't know, it's just something ya wonder. It's not like it's not possible. It happens all the time.

I guess.

Do ya think it matters?

What?

Love.

I don't know—for fuck's sake, Jake, what the hell?

Jake tossed his empty at the garbage can. I think it does. He walked to the door and looked back at Jared. Later.

Yeah, said Jared. Later.

The nightlight is on. Two small beds with just enough room for a dresser between them, pushed back to the wall beneath the only window. Across from the dresser, a closet. It was closed. It's always closed. Especially at night.

Lizzy sleeping on the left side. Zander on the right.

Their father, in the night.

The darkest hour of the night.

The air still, only the faint sounds of their breathing pushing against the sometimes heaviness of being. In the south. This night.

This man.

He reaches his beer to the dresser and misses, the beer running over the scratched strip-wood flooring.

Lizzy wakes, her fear there before her, waiting.

There, and knowing.

She pushes herself away as far as she can, flat to the wall, and she whispers, no. Please, no.

Quiet, her father says, his hand coming to her.

Zander waking.

Just seven years old.

Oh God, no. Please, no.

His hands and his boozy breath, his slurred words, reaching to her. Do not make a fuckin sound.

Oh God, please. Where's the window? She wants the window. Where's the window? Beyond the window.

His hands, finding her, moving over her, and he's making heavy noises.

She squeezes her eyes tight, against the coming pain—she knows only too well. Please, no. No no no. Daddie, please no.

Buster?

Where's the window?

No no, please, no.

Please.

The window?

Please.

Zander slams into his father, and says, don't fucking touch her.

He comes again, and the man backhands the boy across the head knocking him to the ground. What the hell is wrong with you? Are you crazy? Stay the fuck down there, boy. But he doesn't, the man ready, cracking the back of his hand to the boy's head again, the boy out before he hits the floor.

The father's hands pushing and holding, and pushing again. What the fuck is wrong with the two of you?

She can't breathe, the pain, piercing, and she screams. Everything within her, screaming.

Muffled dead screams only she can hear.

Screams only she will ever hear.

Buster? Help me. Please.

And now, only the sad, quiet sounds of a young girl breathing.

The pain there. The pain everywhere.

In that room.

And never will it not be there, and with her.

Never.

The screaming in her head.

Help me, please. Buster.

The tip of the father's knife is wedged between two red-hot stove elements. He looks at his wife, passed out on the couch, the killing of endless maddening moments that cannot touch her now. He removes the knife and walks back to the bedroom. He kneels to the boy's arms, the boy bleeding from his nose and still mostly unconscious. It's time for you to become a man, ya little fucker, and he begins to carve into the boy's forearm the numbers: 18 88 14.

A reminder, you clearly need.

Zander screaming.

So you won't forget, and will always have it.

A reminder, of the ugliness and the dark, this night, that will haunt you, and you will fall to, over and over. Over and over. Like a cloak, that will eventually cover your eyes. A quiet stillness you will seek, and you will find.

Lizzy curled up in a ball and in her mind screaming—no no no. Please, no. Buster, please.

One day, boy, you'll thank me. That's for damn sure, you'll thank me, and don't think you won't.

And now, Lizzy fleeing, in this time, once again, on the back of duskywings.

There's something about the empty town square Finn felt drawn to. The emptiness. Nothing filling in his thoughts for him. The quiet of it, left to remember that which he was pulled to remembering, and could not avoid, or so it seemed. And he knew, there was a sadness to that, one that took him away from life now, these days spent in life remembered, but not as it was, but as he thought it was. For memory most certainly is a poet, as someone said, and not a historian.

Or a jailor, he thought. One or the other.

But we need what we need, and the question is why? And he thinks, come and take us back, Lizzy.

To the woods.

To the river.

All those days ago.

Lizzy, please.

And he heard her say, Finn.

He reached his hands out, to her, in the warm tall grass, his face turning to her. The scent of her. The taste of her. The good feel of her. The sun covering them, and holding them, once again.

And Finn said, today is forever. In this remembering. In this not being.

And in his mind, they slept together, in the tall grass, beneath the warming sun, in that borrowed world.

Borrowed time.

The children tucked in and sleeping, the Monkey King walks in the woods, the moon and the quiet with him, the empty and the dark, and he reaches out to the undercurrent of restless stillness before him, the long reaching sounds of the South. He looks at the moon, his hands in his pockets of not chance—but now. A certainty, he owns. He brings. And he walks on, without thought, unconcerned, and he begins to hum.

At the edge of town he stops.

He walks up the last gravel road before the asphalt streets. He comes to a laneway and walks up it.

He stops and looks at the house.

He enters the house. The woman stretched out on the couch.

At the open bedroom door, he sees Edward there, still in his pants, asleep on top of the blankets.

He bends over the man, titling his head, and Edward wakes, his eyes widening at the sight of the Monkey King's large Black face before him.

The Monkey King wraps his large hand around Edward's neck and squeezes.

Edward kicking. He can't breathe. His hands coming to the Monkey King's hand.

The man is still now, and the Monkey King lifts him, putting him over his shoulder, walking out of the door.

The man's not dead, riding lifeless on the Monkey King's shoulder.

He walks across the yard and opens the small wooden gate and crosses the creek. He comes to a tall pine tree with a broken branch and he lifts the man by his shoulders, holding him out before him, and he says, in my weakness lives the world, and he presses the man to the sharp broken branch, the branch pushing out from the man's chest. He steps back and looks at the man hanging from the tree.

Never again, my dear, Lizzy. Never again.

He walks barefoot, quiet, dark in the dark, through the woods. And now the water, the cold creek water. He's moving in it, and there's a mist, the water rising and coming faster. He stops, standing, looking to the sky, the water breaking to him, rising and moving faster yet, the mist heavier, and like a hell-boy, the sky cracks, rolling in its opening, the desire of lightening welcoming back to itself the source, the wind heavy in it's coming, cracking trees and breaking limbs, big birds flying, and he tilts his head back and opens his mouth and it comes furious, this fury, disastrous and beautiful in its origin, and there, and coming, and always coming harder, and he eats it all.

Upstream, the thin man wearing the straw trilby hat watches.

And in the moving branches of the tress, in the quiet under the moonlight, we hear his voice, once again: You are a child of God too.

He walks on and he plays on, for there is only love, and there is mercy.

PART FIVE

The front of the house is filled with vehicles, mostly police cars and pickup trucks.

The missing children's mother, Kerry, is in the house sitting on the couch surrounded by people, offering their support and comfort.

In the woods, several men stand looking at Edward hanging from the tree.

Why Edward?

Good question. Course there ain't exactly a short list of possibilities, now is there?

They take the body from the branch and place it on the ground and cover it with a yellow plastic sheet.

There were other men and women searching the immediate area, some carrying shotguns or rifles, a few with handguns, walking through the woods, fanned out and calling: Lizzy. Zander. Some with hounds, still on their leashes.

More cars and trucks coming.

Lizzy. Zander.

Helluva thing, ain't it?

Yup, says the sheriff. Ain't it now. Helluva thing.

Lizzy died.

Just like that, she left.

He hadn't noticed.

Why hadn't I?

He didn't know. He didn't know still.

Lizzy, the kids will be home soon, he had told her.

Her body, straight and rigid. Please, she had said, and she said it over and over. Please.

Lizzy?

Please.

Is everything falling away?

No.

Can you feel the sun? That perfect star?

No, I can't. I can't feel it. Make it go away, Finn.

Please, Buster. I'm begging you, make it go away.

In Mackenzie's closet, pushed to the very back.

Lizzy.

Go away, Finn.

In the dark.

You have to come out.

Go away. And she screamed, you don't understand.

Lizzy, I do. Come out, please.

I'm begging you, Finn. Oh, God, please, help me.

Try and feel the water, Lizzy. Try.

I can't, it's not working, make it work. Oh, God, where is he, Finn? Find, Buster, please.

He got up from the town square bench and started walking, needing to push these thoughts away. He really had to. He knew he did, and he tried, over and over, but he couldn't seem to, they just keep coming, like some train on a track in a needle, running, and pushing harder, no matter what.

No matter fucking what.

Tree planting, or not.

So what was the point of that?

You were to leave it in the mountains, with its darkening moving sky. All of it. And not bring it back with you.

It's all just dust, he reminded himself. Nothing more than that. In some place you once walked.

Nothin more.

And don't make it more.

And you weren't always, in bed for weeks at a time, screaming in the night, pulling the curtains down.

Blood flowing.

Not always you weren't.

Not when we were kids.

Not when we had our own kids, especially then, when they were so young and dependent on you. Your endless addiction for them.

Like none other I'd ever seen before.

The inescapable edge of a darkness in a closet.

I could not pull back.

Lizzy?

Please, Lizzy?

I'm beggin ya, Lizzy.

But I didn't notice, you weren't answering.

Lizzy?

Not making any more noises.

I should have noticed.

How come I didn't?

I kept checking for the kids.

You weren't screaming, and you weren't crying anymore.

Lizzy?

And that was it, you were gone.

Just like that, and you were gone.

You'd probably say, Buster thought it was enough, enough pain, enough pushing back against the darkness.

Your duskywings there and with you.

Only the light now and no pain.

And he thought about that.

I'll take a beer, he said.

Blue and red lights, in the dark, flashing. In his mind now.

You're in a butcher shop, said the woman from the café.

Finn turned and looked, and he thought, did I follow you here? I don't think I did? There's a sign, he said, and he pointed back with his thumb toward the front window.

That's next door, said the woman, and she took her packages and change and stopped next to Finn. Come with me.

Her eyes he thought, as he followed her out the door.

Sterling was in his bedroom, a large king size poster bed, a sitting area with a fireplace, bookshelves, a large desk.

He stood at the foot of the bed getting undressed, and he picked up his drink and walked to the French doors and opened them and walked out naked onto the balcony. Naked before Tidewater.

Naked before God.

His father had given him five hundred dollars, worked most of his life saving it up. He looked back, at Marisa cleaning. But he wouldn't go to her, not anymore, not for a long time now.

Not since Loretta died.

The Lord brought a cancer to this house, and she paid for it with her life. Our sins. Not hers.

That's what Marisa had said to him, and she never had him again.

He had told her, that's not right, not the case, He wouldn't do that. But she was ignorant and steadfast in her beliefs, like so many of them were.

I should of fired her.

Maybe I will yet?

He finished his drink and put his hands to the railing and he looked over the town.

His town. A fate joined together. By the grace of God. These Untied Christian States of America, coming.

And coming soon.

On a street in New York City the Quiet Man sat in his parked car, smoking, looking up at a building, just sitting, watching, and waiting, and who would ever know he was there?

No one, and certainly not Jean-Baptiste Duval, not yet in the building.

Finn walked with the woman, looking at her, the streets quiet. She walked light and without hurry.

Thanks for saving me back there.

She looked at Finn, and smiled. You're welcome.

He looked at her more, and he wondered, who are you? What do you know? And will it be enough? And will you tell me what's true and nothing else.

Something, anything but your pain, if you have that too.

Yes, he thought, anything but that.

And they walked more, Finn wondering, still.

I guess the two of you talked about it. Sugar closed the door and walked to the fridge and grabbed a beer.

Not much we did.

Sugar opened her beer. What'd he say?

He wanted to know if it went okay?

And?

Jared bent down and looked at Sugar. And what?

Well, what'd ya say? She pulled herself up onto the high stool at the workbench.

Nothing.

It seemed quieter than normal. Nothin? She looked at the fan. What'ya mean, nothing?

Just that it went okay, that's all. Can we not talk about it.

Why don't ya wanna talk about it?

What's the point?

The point? She crossed her legs, her one foot starting to bounce. Why's it so damn hot in here? What's wrong with that fan? She leaned forward. The point is, we need to figure this out, and right this minute we do.

Jared grabbed a rag and began to wipe his hands. What's with you?

Did you not hear us last night? I'd be surprised if ya didn't.

A little, I did, yeah. What was up? He walked to the fridge and grabbed a beer.

I told him, I ain't no puppy-mill slut, and I ain't sleeping with you no more.

He stopped and looked at Sugar. You're what?

What?

They looked at one another.

You're not sleeping with me no more?

Of course, I am, I just ain't doin it for him no more.

That makes no sense.

Are you dumb? There's a world of difference between my wanting to sleep with you and him wanting me to. And I can tell you this much, we had better figure this out, and I mean soon. She took a sip of his beer. I don't like it, not one bit, do I like it. She took another sip of beer. There's nothing right about this, not a damn thing. Not one.

What'ya mean.

Him saying it's okay for me to sleep with you.

He doesn't want to adopt, that's what he said.

I know that's what he said. But baby, I don't like it, and I'm done talking about it.

Jared looked out the small side window. He looked back at Sugar. I got some money put away.

How much?

Enough.

Good, cause we gotta go, this isn't right, I'm telling ya. She looked at her place. He'll be home soon. She got up, kissed Jared, and walked to the door. She opened it, and looked back. Alice still got inventory down there?

Nope. Sam asked her to help get caught up on some paperwork, and then she went out with Bev.

Stanley?

Yup.

I ran into her last night. We were low on coffee for the morning and I saw her at the store. It was kinda late and she didn't look like she was goin out.

I don't know, I thought that's what she said. Maybe I got it wrong.

The key in the door turned.

Sitting in the dark, waiting, the Quiet Man turned and looked. And what are the thoughts of a Quiet Man in the dark?

Focused knowledge mitigating chance.

He spreads a map on the hood of the Bronco, everyone gathering around.

Right here, this is where I want ya. He circles a spot at an intersection and looks at a tall, thin man named Zeke. There's a store. A blonde'll be coming out at noon. She's the one. He looks at a man next to Zeke, not too rough, but make it good. He looks back at Zeke. The sheriff knows to be there for noon. Same as always, out on bail in no time and you know the rest. He looks at several men to the back of the group. Truman and Richard, I don't want anyone hurt on that liquor store. Understood?

As long as there's no heroes pulling guns, there won't be.

Either way, keep it clean, otherwise, it's just—difficult. All right, that's it.

They sat outdoors in the cool night air. There was no one else. They waited for their drinks, not speaking, looking at one another, trying to see all that they could see of one another under the distant light of the midnight sun.

Their drinks came and they sipped them. Finn unable to take his eyes from her, her pale skin in the dim light, her green eyes, present and yet distant, with their own particular slant to them. Far away and remembering. How do you know my name? he asked her.

Tidewater.

Tidewater?

Yes, but we can talk about that later, if you like. Let's just sit here. It's such a beautiful night.

All right, but you can at least tell me your name.

Isabelle.

That's a nice name.

Is it? I don't like it.

I'm trying to place the name.

Isabelle Honey. It might come to you, but I doubt it. I'm younger. Why are you here?

Me?

Yes.

Working. I'm on a bus back tomorrow.

Are you?

Yes.

I've often wondered what it would be like to go back.

How long have you been gone? asked Finn.

A long time, but there are parts of it I'll never forget.

I bet. It's a hard place to forget. Even when you want to. Maybe even more so then.

Yes, I think so too. It certainly is its own strange, particular place, isn't it?

He looked south. Yes, he said, it is.

The children are tucked in still, beneath the bearskin. Zander sleeping, not Lizzy. The Monkey King sitting next to them, stretching his legs out, crossing his feet.

I hope it doesn't take too long.

What's that, Lizzy?

California.

Oh, I dunno. I guess it might. It's pretty far.

I know I call you Buster, but what's your real name?

Isidore.

Oh, I like that.

Thank you. But you can still call me Buster. I have lots of names.

No, I think Isidore is just fine.

Do you? Ok then, that's it. Isidore it is.

Lizzy smiles. Isidore. Where are you from?

Here.

Tidewater?

No.

She waits, and when he doesn't say anything more, she says, Zander doesn't mean to be rude ya know. He's not really.

I know he's not.

He's just mad.

I know.

He rips things, all sorts of things.

He does?

Yup, and he sleeps with a garden tool.

A garden tool?

Some sharp weedy thing.

What about you?

Me?

Yeah, how do you feel about going to California?

I'll miss it here, a little bit. I know I'm not supposed to, but I will.

That's all right, Lizzy, there's nothing wrong with that. We never know what's coming next, do we?

No, I guess that's right.

Do you remember the river, Lizzy? The water running over us and the rocks beneath us?

Lizzy smiles. Yes.

Like that.

And the sun.

Yes, and the sun, too, and he tilts his head back and closes his eyes, his face warming to the good feel of an imagined sun. Everything's falling away, Lizzy. Can ya feel it? Can you remember that?

She doesn't answer, and he looks down, at Lizzy's sleeping.

A smile on her face.

Lizzy.

Beautiful little Lizzy.

Flying away, somewhere—somewhere safe, on her duskywings, once again.

Ya wanna go somewhere? Cael asked Mackenzie.

Where, there's nowhere to go.

We could go to the river.

They started to walk at the side of the road, not really going anywhere, just walking.

I wanna go home, said Mackenzie.

Now?

No, I mean our home.

Oh?

Don't you miss it?

Yeah, I guess, said Cael. I like it here though too.

That's just because you don't have any friends back home.

Yes, I do.

Who?

Lots.

I miss mine, and I wanna go home, and he better take us.

He said he would.

I hope so, we been here too long already.

It's not that bad.

She looked at Cael. What do you know?

I know enough, like why Dad left.

Well, I know that too. It's not some big mystery.

No, I guess not. Do you think of her?

Yeah. What I remember.

Me too, and I remember lots. I miss her.

I do too.

Are you just saying that? Do you remember enough to even miss her?

I remember enough—well, one thing really.

What?

She was lying next to me, and she said she loved me, and to always remember that. And that if she ever went away, it wouldn't be because of me. Or you.

Yeah, she told me that too. She killed herself, you know. In my closet.

Cael doesn't answer, and he looks towards the hill he likes to climb. The long line of railroad tracks. The stones he likes to throw, standing above the town; this town, he is only starting to get to know, and where he doesn't feel as lonely, as he has before. He looked back at his sister. I don't want to leave her when he comes back.

You don't? I do.

I know you do. He will too. But I don't.

Well, too bad for you, and she pushed her brother, and ran away.

You're a miserable little shit, Mackenzie Finlay, that's what you are.

That's what you say, Mackenzie called back.

Yup, that's what I say, and he ran after his sister.

He stopped before he closed the door and turned the light on. Who the fuck are you?

This won't take long.

Get the hell out.

Sit down.

I'm calling the cops.

You should probably just sit down, said the Quiet Man, and listen to what I have to say.

Jean-Baptiste Duval closed the door and walked forward. Who the fuck are you and what do you want?

The Quiet Man slid the manila envelope across the table.

Jean-Baptiste Duval sat down and picked it up. What is it?

He nodded forward.

Jean-Baptiste Duval opened it and began to read the document. He looked up.

The Quiet Man reached into the breast pocket of his coat and pulled out a bank draft and placed it on the table.

He reached forward and looked at it. A million dollars.

Sign the paper and it's yours. The Quiet Man reached again into his coat pocket and dropped a pen on the table. He leaned closer, if you violate one term of the agreement, a single call, one text, any public mention of your relationship to either Hunter, or Amanda, you'll void the agreement, and that, he leaned back in his chair, would not be to your benefit.

Jean-Baptiste Duval looked again at the document. He flipped through it, reading. He looked back at the bank draft and picked up the pen and signed the document and handed it to the Quiet Man. Now get the fuck out.

In his office, only the desk light on, Sterling leaned back in his chair and took a sip of whiskey. His phone rang and he reached back to his desk and picked it up and put it to his ear. Un-huh, good.

I'll be back soon, said the Quiet Man.

Sterling flipped his phone shut and put it back on the desk and thought, one less problem to worry about.

Jared pulled his pickup over next to the Piggly Wiggly parking lot and put it in park, the engine running beneath the outer edge of light coming from the nearest streetlight.

Her car was there.

Fuck, he said, and he lit a cigarette. He smoked and he thought, what's it matter now?

Dumb bitch.

It doesn't.

I'm out, anyway. The sooner the better.

But still, fuck her, and he turned the wheel and drove away.

Not like that. Here.

Cael watched his grandfather show him the knot again, two desert plates on the table next to them, both with forks and bits of pie crumbs left on them.

Have you talked to your father lately?

Cael nodded.

He's coming home.

Yup, in a few days.

Are you excited?

Still watching his grandfather's hands, Cael said, yes.

You'll be going back to your house. Here, you try.

Cael took the fishing line and tried tying the knot on the hook.

I bet Mackenzie's looking forward to it, and he smiled, and Cael smiled too.

I'll miss you and Grandmother.

Why? Because your dad can't cook like your grandmother?

Cael looked at his grandfather and smiled again. Yup.

His grandfather tousled Cael's hair and said, don't you worry, you'll be seeing plenty of us, and I'm sure your grandmother will still be cookin you all sorts of good things.

Like her lemon meringue pie?

Would you like another piece?

Yes, please.

Make it two pieces, said Cael's grandfather.

Did you and Lizzy end up together?

Yes.

I'm glad you did. Kids?

Two. Mackenzie and Cael.

You must miss them?

I do, Finn said, and he looked at the rim of the midnight sun, all that was left of it, and back again, south of that, where he'd be back soon. He looked at Isabelle and held up his empty glass. Another one?

Yes, thank you.

Finn flagged the waitress and indicated two more.

When you walked into the butcher shop, said Isabelle, I couldn't believe it. At the diner I thought, it couldn't be. But at the butcher shop, once you spoke, I knew it was you.

Quite the first impression?

She smiled.

I saw you at the diner.

The waitress brought their drinks and Finn paid.

I know you did, I thought you might have recognized me, you were looking so hard.

Was I?

Yes.

I didn't.

Are you Dr. Honey's daughter? The big yellow house on the corner?

It's yellow?

Yeah.

It wasn't then, it was white.

That's what people still say, Doc Honey's place.

It's nice that people remember that.

When did you leave?

Not long after they found Lizzy and Zander. My father couldn't stay after that—well, he tried, but—poor Lizzy.

You knew Lizzy?

I remember her, of course, coming and going from my father's office. His examine room. School, a little bit. Whatever happened to Zander?

Overdose.

Oh, I'm so sorry. I liked him.

Me too. Their father did a real number on them both, despite what people think.

Still?

Yes.

My father began to drink. He couldn't stay there, it was killing him, and so we came here, about as far away as you could get. He tried. He really did, but it didn't work. He couldn't leave it behind him, but I guess that's not so uncommon, is it?

No, I guess not.

They sipped their drinks, not speaking. Tidewater on their minds.

He was the biggest man I've ever seen. He was a giant. They brought him in so my dad could look at his wounds, which were horrible and disgusting. I think they were worried he might die before they had a chance to execute him. My dad said he'd never seen another man like him. I peeked through the examination room door one time. I was terrified. He saw me and smiled and winked and his whole face lit up. I'll never forget it. Did you not see him when they brought into town?

Yeah, I saw.

In chains, dragged behind a pickup like that.

Finn didn't answer.

I've often thought about him. Lizzy, too, and, of course, Zander, and how lucky they were to have known him.

I don't know, said Finn.

No?

He was always with her, and she couldn't let go.

How do you mean?

I don't know.

It breaks my heart, even now to think about it. Do people still talk about it?

No. Never.

Do people still think—.

Yes. As far as I can tell. But I don't care. I did once.

It wasn't him.

No? said Finn. According to your father it was.

That's not fair. It destroyed him.

I guess it would.

They forced him.

Did they?

Yes.

I'm sorry. It was a long time ago. We should just forget about it. He looked at her, at the small silver ring in her nose, at how beautiful she was, how he could feel himself falling into her, and he thought, ghosts fly—make that happen.

All of them.

It's the eyes, he tells himself. Taking him. Can they hold him? Yes, he thought, there's such a depth to them. But there's something else. What? He didn't know. Like him, just like that, or so it seemed to him. But they shouldn't, for she does not know, he's a marked, and failed man, having fallen from the folds of time—of this life, yesterday. In the here now, too. And what of tomorrow?

Lizzy told my father it wasn't him.

I know.

They wouldn't listen to him, my father, and they threatened him. I heard the conversation, although, he never spoke of it.

She was too emotionally distraught. Too unstable. Too young. That's what they said.

It was all so horrible. The trial—.

I know. Finn looked away. It didn't stop there.

No?

He looked back at Isabelle. They continued to discredit her in everything she ever did, or said, after that. Like it was her fault, somehow. Like she was deranged to even suggest—.

That it was her father?

Yes.

It's so disgusting. What he did. What they all did, to cover it up, and blame him, and then—what they did to him.

Far more—believable—acceptable, somehow, if it was a Black man. What white man would ever do that to their own daughter?

And still no one says anything?

No.

Poor Lizzy. I can't imagine it.

She said it didn't matter. He would always be there.

Did she?

Yes.

Can I ask you something?

Sure.

After your parents took them in, with their mom being—.

Dead too?

Yes. Is that when you—.

Fell in love?

Yes.

We were just kids, the same age, and Zander was, not mean, he was never mean, but he had an edge to him, at times, a hard one, and my father spent a lot of time with him, which was good, and Lizzy and I, we just had lots of time on our own, to do just that—fall in love. And we did. We were never not together. It was like that, and we never questioned it. Never wanted to. No one else ever did, either. Like it was meant to happen.

I wish I had known her better.

You'd have liked her. I wish we'd been like you.

Oh?

Yes.

How so?

Moved.

Do you?

Yes.

Do you think it would have made a difference?

No. It would have been like your father.

She looked away.

But it wouldn't have been in her face all the time so much, either. Never getting away from it. But we did eventually leave, as soon as we were married, and could.

Are you glad you did?

Yes, but the damage had been done, and there was no escaping that.

Her father?

Yes.

Did he kill her father? asked Isabelle.

Isidore?

Yes.

Yes, I think so, and I'm glad he did.

Me too. Would you like to go now?

Where?

You can walk me home, if you like.

Yes, I'd like that. They stood, and she took his hand, and they began to walk.

With the coming of dark they ended the search for that day. Some had lingered, but were gone now too.

Kerry was alone in the house for the first time, with the quiet, the shadows of the woods on her mind.

She couldn't settle, and she walked out onto the porch. In the dark. She sat on the top step, feeling as if she was coming out of her skin.

This wasn't her world.

No, none of it.

Who she was. Who she was meant to be.

And Edward?

Dead now, and it's all too late, anyway, they're gone. All of them. And damn him.

She wondered more. What had she done?

Too late for any of it. Too late for her. She had her chances. She knew she did. Lizzy. Zander. I'm so sorry. She looks down at Edward's gun in her lap, and she looks back to the woods, where she knows they are. Where she knows she can't go. She puts the gun to her head. Don't come back, either one of you, do you understand?

Ever.

No matter what.

Promise me you won't, and she pulls the trigger.

They sat in Jake's pickup at the big bend on the river just past town.

It gives me pause, said Amanda, every time, just how beautiful it is.

The wide river rippling slow before them in the moonlight. The long shadows of the great trees.

Why'd ya come back?

I told you, for Hunter.

That's it? Just for him?

She took a sip of beer and looked at the river. Hunter's father and I have had our problems, you might say. She looked at Jake. What about you?

Me?

You and Sugar?

He looked at Amanda. We can't have kids.

Oh, I'm sorry, Jake.

It's me. I got tested.

Really? So all that fussing and worrying back in high school was for nothing?

Jake laughed. I guess it was.

How's Sugar taking it?

He finished his beer and leaned his arm over the seat and dropped his empty. She's been sleeping with my brother for the past year. That's how she's taking it.

Jared?

Yup, and he opened a new beer.

Amanda, leaning her head against his shoulder, said, people can be so shitty.

I don't know. It's hard, I guess, knowing sometimes what's the right thing to do, and what's not. Like you, when you didn't come back.

I cried endlessly.

I should have left right away to find you.

I couldn't do it, I tried, but I was never going to be Sterling Spalding's little Miss Tidewater, or Jake Burleson's all-star football sweetheart. It wasn't in me.

We didn't have to stay here.

Oh, please, she lifted her head, you were born, bred and true, and you know it.

I suppose I was, then. He looked back at Amanda. I'm not now.

No?

I don't think so, no.

They continued looking at one another, falling back, slow and unsure, and they kissed, and they kissed more, and longer yet.

The light of the moon finding them.

Just them.

That night.

Falling back to missed time.

Zander.

What is it Lizzy?

We should go home now.

In a minute.

It's getting dark.

I know it.

What'ya doin?

Never mind, says Zander. Play with your friends.

They had to go home, it was getting dark, and they'd be in trouble. Just like us.

I didn't go home, Lizzy.

Oh, Buster, I didn't see you there. I'm glad you didn't go.

I'm still looking for that one button, and I know it came off here somewhere.

It doesn't matter, Buster. It wasn't your fault.

We could sew it back on, if we could find it. It's not too dark, yet. It's gotta be here somewhere.

It's all right.

Oh no, Lizzy, I'd like to find it, it's gotta be here? It's a good button, and you might get in trouble.

I won't get in trouble, Buster, but you look for it more if you want to, I gotta go home. Zander?

Lizzy, do you think it came off when we were more over here?

I don't know, Buster, I didn't notice. Zander? We gotta go. You know what'll happen. You can catch more crawfish tomorrow.

I'm coming, Lizzy—goddamnit, it's dark already.

Thanks for staying and lookin for that one button, Buster. Buster?

Forget your damn friends, Lizzy, we gotta go. We're late now.

Keep the gate open—and he keeps the gate open, and they run, the water guarding the woods.

There's just so many, look at em all. I'd better tell Zander.

Lizzy?

It's so very lovely this morning, with the sun, the water so warm and shallow, I could sit right down in it.

Lizzy. Come and have some breakfast.

There's crawfish over there, lots of em.

Zander already got some. C'mon now.

I'll be right there, Isidore, one minute.

Don't be too long.

And she leans back to the water, her arms stretching back above her head, the water running over her, the sun warming her face, and she closes her eyes—all the big birds flying, and now her, too, on the back of her duskywings.

Would you like a turn runnin the trains, Hunter?

The boy nodded and they got up from the table and walked down the long arched hallway, Hunter taking his grandfather's hand.

There was just something so right about it, thought Sterling. This boy—his grandson, with him now. Like another chance, he thought. God's doing.

Of course, it was.

One, he thought, he had most certainly earned. And he wouldn't let others get in the way of that, not this time.

No matter who they were.

Or what they thought.

The boy had to be made right, that was clear.

And like a sadness heard echoing, coming back through time—all of our time, over and over, they walked, hand-in-hand, down the long hallway.

This is turnin out to be one helluva shitstorm.

They were looking down at Kerry's skull and her brain scattered on the worn porch boards.

In the cold hard light of daytime.

In that particular, still and quiet heat.

I guess them kids are orphans now, says the deputy.

The sheriff looks at the deputy. If we find em.

With a murderer among them, there were more people turning out for the hunt, more men in pickups with rifles searching the roads, more people fanning out in the woods, some with dogs, more women staying behind having brought food and comfort.

We don't know for sure they have them, a woman says.

That's right, we have to stay positive, says another woman.

I can't stand to think about it, not after—well, you know, what they done to Edward.

A woman lowers her voice, leaning toward the other women. I heard it might be one of them.

I heard it too.

Wouldn't surprise me, would it surprise you?

No.

Imagine?

Horrible.

And poor Kerry. Losing her entire family, like that.

Who could blame her?

No, that's right.

Lord have mercy.

Those people.

Those damn people.

Lord, save our souls.

Humble before God.

What'd I tell ya? and Sugar pulled herself up onto the stool and crossed her legs, her wrist hanging over her knee, an opened beer in her hand. How long?

How long what? asked Jared.

How long has Alice been sleeping with him?

How should I know?

Oh, for God's sake, you didn't say anything to her, did ya?

Nope, and Jared went back to work on a motor part.

Sugar took a sip of beer. You're such a Burleson, aren't ya? She leaned back, her elbows on the workbench. When are we goin? And don't tell me you're putting that off too?

Not long now, that's for damn sure. I got a few things I gotta take care of first.

Like what?

Like, it won't take long, that's how long.

I can't wait, that's all. I'm anxious. She put her beer on the workbench. Why don't ya come over here and leave that old car thing alone? We got time yet.

Jared put the car part down and wiped his hands with a rag. He threw the rag on the workbench and picked up Sugar's beer and took a sip. How long we been together?

I don't know. She took her beer back. A few years now, why?

Jared walked to the fridge and grabbed a beer and walked back. He leaned against the workbench and drank his beer. In all this time we been doin it, were ya never worried about getting pregnant? Or were ya just hoping ya would, and say it was Jake's?

Sugar turned on her stool and looked at Jared, her head tilting, her blonde hair hanging down to the side. Are you out of your mind? You don't get it, do ya? All this damn talk of babies, I can't hardly take it.

What'ya mean?

Sugar put her beer down and got up from her stool and began to pace in her flip-flops, Jared watching her, in her tight jeans, her white ribbed t-shirt, tight and cut low. She stopped and looked at Jared. It's the last thing I'm ever gonna do, do you understand that?

What?

This world is a hard world, Jared Burleson, and it gets no easier being woman, that's for damn sure. She picked up her beer and took a sip. And if you think I'm gonna get dropped down another rung by having either yours or your brother's damn babies, ya gotta another thing comin. Besides, it plays absolute havoc with your body, destroys it completely. She looked at Jared. Is that what you want?

Hold on, are you telling me all this time you've been on birth control?

That is correct, smart boy, yes I have.

And all this time Jake thought you were trying to get pregnant?

Correct.

And then it turns out, he's sterile. What would ya have done if he hadn't been?

I don't know. I'd of figured somethin out.

And now he has me doin you to get ya pregnant, even though I already am, and you're on birth control?

As it turns out, yes.

Fuck, Sugar. Don't ya think that's a little crazy?

I have not one idea about that, not one. To be honest, I try not to concern myself with such things.

Jared laughed. Come here, Sugar, and he pulled her to him.

Let's just go, baby, please. I can't take it much longer. Honest to God, I can't.

No, that's right, he said, neither can I, and he kissed her, his hands finding her—her curves, the good lines of her.

And she said, baby, yes, like that.

Just like that. And the sooner we go, the better.

I know it, he said. Not long.

In that county for three days, they did their work well.

Zeke and two others at the store at the appropriate hour.

The blonde woman with a grocery bag in her arms exiting at noon, walking the length of the covered porch. The hard, mid-day sun washing everything else away.

Zeke stepped forward.

Two other men approaching from the back of the woman.

She stops.

Two elderly women walking down the road stop.

A man pulling up in a pickup stops. He puts the truck in park, the engine running. He doesn't get out.

Zeke stretches his arm out, his hand finding the building, blocking the woman's path.

She tries to turn the other way, the other two men there, and she stops, her groceries dropping to the sidewalk.

The older women on the road put their hands to their mouths.

The pickup door begins to open, and Zachery's men turn and look, and the man closes the door.

Zeke's hand finds the back of the woman's thigh. She screams, trying to push away. His hand now, moving up her leg, as he backs her against the wall.

She brings her fist down on him.

Bitch, and he pins her to the building.

She's crying—please.

A woman with a young boy appears at the store door.

The men on the porch turn and look.

An older man, the owner of the store, appears with a shotgun in his hands, and Zeke's two men step forward, their guns pointed at the man's head, and he, too, steps back.

Zeke looks at the woman's breasts, and he rips her dress away, his other hand still under her dress.

The sheriff's car pulls up, its lights flashing, and it stops. The sheriff and a deputy step out, their guns ready. The sheriff tells the men on the porch, put the guns down. Right the fuck now.

One of the two men steps toward the woman and puts his gun to her head. I don't think so.

Zeke turns his gun on the sheriff.

Let her go, says the sheriff, cause I got no problem with you bein dead right now.

Zeke smiles. C'mon, Sheriff Hector, there's no need for violence, she's my girlfriend. He looks at the woman. Aren't ya, baby?

The woman shakes her head, no.

She's just being shy.

The sheriff and the deputy step forward.

Fine, sheriff, settle down. Have it your way, and he motions for the other two to drop their guns.

They do, tossing them onto the road.

You too, Hector tells Zeke.

Zeke drops his gun, whispering to the woman as he does, and I was just about to make you my girlfriend for real.

The woman whispers back, and you could have too.

On your knees, assholes, says the deputy. I said, on your knees, and he shotgun butts the one man in the head. He looks at the other man. You, too, and he shotgun butts him.

Black man blood running and pooling, on the warm sidewalk boards.

The sheriff holsters his gun and removes his baton, and he says, and what makes you think you shouldn't be on your knees? And he takes Zeke down with a blow to the legs.

Due justice.

This is ours, and it ain't ever gonna be ours, due justice.

A boot finds Zeke's ribs, another one his face. The sheriff puts his hand on the deputy's arm. That's probably good.

They handcuff the men and drag them to the car.

They jacked cars, these paid men of Zachery's, where they stood, at gunpoint, under the hot sun, not caring who saw, the more the better. And they lingered downtown, loitering and panhandling, harassing people, offering to buy drugs, sell drugs. At night they fought one another in bars, waiting for others to step in, and then they fought them too.

In the liquor store, one of Zachery's men held a gun to a customer's head. C'mon, do it, it's your right, what are ya waitin for? He pressed his .38 against the man's head, the man wearing a checkered cotton short-sleeve shirt tucked into khaki pants, a brown belt and brown shoes, a comb in his shirt pocket, and he was wearing glasses, his hand held just above his open carry weapon. Just a couple no-good porch cats prowling around in here, ain't that right? What'ya gonna do about it? You gonna let your daddie down and his daddie too? Is that what ya gonna do? Hell no, you ain't gonna do that, c'mon now, boy, be the hero. Take these niggas down.

The man's shaking hand lowers, the others in the liquor store watching.

What could possibly go wrong? You're on the side of right—white is right, and you know it, and I know it, and little baby Jesus on the wall over there, He knows it too. So? Daddie's watchin, what'ya gonna do?

And the man does, he pulls his gun, and as he does, he takes a .38 to the head.

Zachary's men laughing. Dumb-ass Cracker.

The man, Richard, at the counter holding up the store owner, having turned and looked, doesn't see the owner reaching under the counter for his sawed-off side-by-side. He fires.

Truman turns and looks, and he does, the store owner shoots him too.

A tall thin man with greasy dark hair standing with the other customers watching, says, them's two dead niggers now.

Zachery was employed by Hector, who was employed by Sterling Spalding, for years now. Agitators. A steady gig, from town-to-town.

This unleashing.

This—our world, defined and shaped by us, and only us.

Not women, either. Never that.

By God's hand.

And that's what they thought, and did still, for the most part.

Humble before God.

Praise Jesus.

Hunter ran the trains, his little, slightly off-colored hand, on the box.

Steady now, said Sterling, his hand coming to the boy's hand, and he pointed, keep an eye on the engine, and watch what's coming up ahead. You need to anticipate. Be ready. You're in control. That's it. You're the conductor. Slow and steady now. You need to find the right rhythm and pace, set the tone, you alone, you're the one. You're a Sterling.

Goddamnit, Hunter, steady now.

Slow down.

Hunter.

Goddamnit.

The trains crashed, the boy running from the room.

Hunter, said his grandfather. Get the hell back here. We don't quit.

His mother was standing at the open door.

Jesus Christ.

Hunter in his mother's arms, crying.

That's enough, Dad. Leave him alone. And she walked away with her son.

She died, right there in the closet, just like that. Like she just left.

I'm sorry, Finn.

She'd suffered enough.

Maybe it was Isidore?

It's nice to think so, isn't it?

They were walking, and it was getting lighter, and Finn looked past Isabelle, at the light of the rising sun. Of a new day coming. One that would see him on a bus back to his kids. Some money in his pocket, and back home with them. All the blood—running, all the memories, left in the mountains, and they could start again. Him and just the kids. He knew they could. He just needed to get home to them. Soon. Not long now.

He looked back at Isabelle, and thought, but what of you?

Sterling Spalding was at his desk in his library. The Quiet Man standing at the tall window looking out past the heavy pulled curtains.

She's gonna be a problem, ya know that, right?

The Quiet Man didn't look back.

Not the boy, though, we can still put him right. There's time yet for that. What does she know about this world? Nothing. Born into it, without a single idea of what it takes. Not one. Lying herself down for—for fuck's sake. He swiveled around in his chair. I don't even like to think about it.

The Quiet Man looked down at Sterling, and said, don't.

No, that's right. It doesn't help. We'll fix it soon enough. All of it. And fucking soon we will.

By God's will.

Yes, said Sterling. By God's hand. He looked back at the Quiet Man. By the way, I didn't ask. Was he very Black? Or just a little?

Black enough, said the Quiet Man.

The old man with the beautiful olive skin wearing a trilby hat was walking, and he stops. In the distance, He sees rain. He looks around. He looks back. The Monkey King is standing before him. Lizzy and Zander too.

Where are you goin? the old man asks.

California, says Lizzy.

Oh, California. Go back.

Why? asks Zander.

It's far and what you're looking for is not there.

Who said we're lookin for anything, says Zander.

There's not a soul alive who's not. Go back. The man looks back to the horizon. She has eyes that are all the world's light. She keeps all the rain for me. Have ya seen her?

Who? asks Lizzy.

The Monkey King smiles.

Go back. There's lots of people lookin. Lots. I'll find her. He tips his trilby hat and walks on.

Who was that? asks Lizzy.

The Monkey King looks back.

He's a little strange, says Zander.

There's little that's strange, Zander. Someone once said, love pours life into death and death into life without a drop being spilled. Perhaps it was him?

I liked him, says Lizzy.

Yes, me, too, says the Monkey King.

I don't know, says Zander. I still think he's a little strange.

The Monkey King laughs, his all-the-world laugh, and they walk on.

On their way to California.

They turned right and walked up a dark laneway. Isabelle stopping. Through the mostly pulled curtains of a window on a corner townhouse they saw an old man asleep in a chair. A bottle of whiskey and a glass on a reading table next to him.

Finn looked at Isabelle. It's amazing how one thing in life can destroy you. Even when you know it's happening to you, and you can't, or won't, do anything about it.

Yes, she said.

I'm sorry, said Finn.

It's okay. He's been like that for a long time now. C'mon, we can go this way.

Sterling was standing at the window, the Quiet Man no longer there, and he thought, we're close. He took a sip of whiskey. And thank the good Lord for that. It's been a long time coming.

Too long.

The United Christian States of America.

And what a beautiful thing it will be.

Goddamnit, finally. All these years now.

A sovereign-association of morals; of understanding; of respect. One hundred and thirty-seven counties across three states of the most beautiful land in this torn apart, once great nation.

It's the way—the only way forward.

A nation under God.

How we ever thought there could be another way, I don't know?

Everything so misguided and wrong. The state of things.

Gone too far.

In God we trust and always will.

Something we all knew at one point, and forgot. All of us.

And then, what were we left with? Too many weak, non-deserving, pathetic souls.

That's the damn problem.

Or was—because, why should that be our concern?

It's not.

Not anymore, and he opened the window, to the quiet night air. Why should we, strong in our conviction, not live a life true to His word, and only His word? Why should we not be allowed to? Do we not have a moral obligation?

That's clear. Of course, we do, and it makes no sense not to fulfill it to the best of our abilities.

Even if others can't, or won't.

And goddamnit, we won't be held hostage.

Not again.

Not ever again.

And we won't be denied.

Not now.

Not ever.

His will is our will.

God's voice in America.

Humble before God.

Praise Jesus.

These United Christian States of America.

Coming soon, and not soon enough. He finished his whiskey, and he said to the town below him—his town, and it's all for you, and you are welcome.

Jake stopped. He was early for work. The pickup running, and he looked up to the Sterling estate, wanting to believe it could hold together, but he was unsure of that. Amanda, he said.

Live and love and learn.

Or don't.

He turned the truck around and drove to the mill.

They were fishing, the young boy and his grandfather, and a warm breeze came up, and the old man, closing his eyes, leaned his face to it, the boy watching, and he saw a smile come to the old man's face, and he liked that, it made him good, and he thought, he wished he could climb right up there, right now, with the old man, and stay there, like that, always, and together they could watch the old man's time drifting there before them on the lazy, shaded river, real and gone, and there again, for his grandfather to pluck at and say—see, it's right there, still all right there, when I was just boy, like you. And in this, there would be contentment, without meaning, in the honest days of a life. In the days of a life still to come. As if in a dream that could only be found by young boy climbing up through the worn, threadbare buttonhole of an old man's sweater.

This suggestion of love, under a big moon, by a lazy, shaded river. There, and with us always.

These forever Tidewater skies.

Squatting next to a stream, Lizzy and Zander were floating sticks, watching, not speaking, the sun not yet all the way up, and it was quiet, and they weren't really wondering about anything. Just living, in this world now. In themselves. The Monkey King's voice coming to them. Come along, now. It's time to go.

And they did, and they walked more, on their way to the endless sunny blue skies of California.

Just kids, and not fully broken. Not fully broken yet, by all of our beliefs.

Amanda was watching Hunter swimming, and she poured another glass of sangria. Her phone lit up with a message. Money deposited, it read. She put the phone back on the table, and she took another sip.

He drove through town, this town that wasn't his anymore, not really. It might look the same, it hadn't changed all that much, but it had enough. If you knew where to look.

That's for damn sure.

It wasn't the town of his days, football, and endless summers, people lookin the other way—toe the line, boy, and you'll be fine. Bring it home. There was still plenty—too much for his liking, of the old holdover, the ugly undertones, but they stayed mostly buried, and people got along, for the most part, they found a way. People just lookin to just get by. That was hard enough. There might be a whisper, or a look, maybe a word or two, but that was it. The law ran its own way—it always did, but ya knew that line too. If you were from here, you did. At least back then. Perhaps, not anymore. It's all changed. So why stay? What's here? Nothin, that's what. It's all a new line, all the free zones gone—where you could really find a life, all of it shut down and sucked dry by their self-righteousness. The goddamn religious right and their ideas of a better life; a better heaven, for you and me. Their damn fears. He looked back over his shoulder. All of it flamed on by you. Your inflated ego. Your goddamn money.

He entered the gate at the mill and parked, and with his lunchbox in his hand, he exited his truck, and he walked into the mill.

Fuck em, he thought. I'm still a free man, and I've got some backbone left, yet.

Finn's parents, in the early warmth of the evening, walked the riverbank, as they had so many times before, the current slow and easy, the overhanging trees and their Spanish moss sheltering them. She took his arm, the weight of his shoulder next to her, and she did not want her thoughts becoming words. Not this night. She looked up to the arco de la estrella of the town's first cemetery. The image of that night coming as it so often did lately. Poor Lizzy. What it did to her. What it did to Finn. That poor man. She looked at her husband. This place has much to atone for, one day. And I hope I'm not here to see it.

Are you feeling unsettled?

Yes, a little.

Lizzy?

All of them.

Should we turn around?

She nodded. Let's get away from the river.

Anything you'd like to talk about?

She looked at her husband. I'll feel better once Finn gets home.

Yes, I will as well.

They walked up a set of stone stairs, and she said, let's just sit awhile.

And they did, on a bench overlooking the bay. The night upon them. The moon there.

Do you remember?

He looked to where she was looking. A long wooden building on high wooden stilts overhanging the bay. Long shutdown now. Yes, he said.

All those nights.

Yes.

It's like there's two worlds, isn't there?

How so?

Well, like those nights back then. Nights, and days, of such rarified air. Our hopes and our dreams. The certainty of expectations. This world of ours. She looked now at the low cinderblock building next to the closed nightclub. A café with graffiti on the walls. Scrubby bushes running along the side of it. Here name was Beatrice. The waitress.

I remember. We were at the club that night.

Yes. So sad and so horrible. But that's what I mean. Because there's that world too. Submerged. Our hands upon it, keeping it that way. She took his arm in hers, and she placed her head on his shoulder. See it or not, that's the sad truth of it, and always has been.

They found her in the bay, the next morning.

Yes.

Her father—.

Let's not talk about it.

Do you think we should have left?

She looked up to Sterling's house, high up on the hill. If he has his way, we most certainly will.

He looked too. Oh, that. You don't think—.

Yes, I do. She looked at her husband. I don't see how he won't be successful. His money. His way. And all those that follow.

Well, if he does, I'm with you. There'll be no tolerating this place then.

It's shameful, and it's a disgrace. This narrowing. And so widespread, and embraced with such conviction. As if there wasn't even a chance they might be wrong. Or, not right.

Too many people now, lost to the same fears. What was it your father used to say?

Try not to tie your ideological blindfolds too tight.

He smiled. Right. And all too true.

There's entire generations now—like Finn, and the kids, that have never known anything else. Just the slow destruction of what a society can be—or was, at one time, and I miss it, so terribly much, I miss it. And I wonder, will it ever change?

He looked out over the bay. As I do. Miss it. He looked back at his wife. Speaking of Finn and the kids, maybe that's where we should go?

Sell the store?

Why not? It's been long enough, don't you think?

It would be nice to be close to them, and she put her head back on his shoulder, and said, yes, let's do that.

They looked at the moon on the bay. Their love for one another there and with them.

Under a big moon. By a big, shady river.

Tidewater, USA.

We let it happen, he said, and he looked back up at Sterling's house, high up on the hill. All of us.

Yes, she said, it's true. All of us.

He was sitting up on a large white oak branch overhanging the river, His legs crossed, a cigarette burning down between his fingers, His trilby tipped forward, and he began to hum a hymn of hope to the rhythm of the current.

I know you're out there, and I'll find you yet. I always do. He smoked more, and he hummed more, and he looked at the older couple sitting looking out at the moon on the bay. True love, he said. It's the only way forward. Isn't that right, Fate, my darling?

And good for Isidore, he thought, helping those kids out. They'll need it. He'll do right by them, of course, he will, and he looked back to the horizon. He's a good boy. A good son. And he hummed on, to the horizon. For all time—all of it, there now, before him.

They will slaughter him like a dog.

A fuckin dog.

Fuckin same.

Worse than a dog.

Like he done to Edward.

Damn right, like he done to Edward.

One pickup, the side of the road, six men with shotguns and rifles, drinking beer to the line that rings, and rings harder yet. These men with guns raging at the cold hard taste of metal in their mouths, they did not put there, or understand, or want to.

And this man's blood, it will come, it will run, to the darkening sky, to the damp heavy earth, running over their boots, warm and slow from their forever hands.

And don't think it won't always, be just like this.

Cause it will.

Hate spilling blood at the beckoning of fear.

Our fear, giving away to a hate that kills.

Fear that burns, and it burns still.

I'm tired, says Lizzy.

Zander looks at Lizzy. But we haven't gone very far yet. Hardly at all.

We could go back to my camp, says the Monkey King, it's not far at all, and we could sleep the night there.

If we do that, we'll have wasted all day, says Zander.

We had fun though, says the Monkey King. Did we not?

We did, says Lizzy. I liked it. I could spend every day in these woods, just like that, with only the two of you, forever.

Me too, Lizzy, says the Monkey King.

But we're not in California, says Zander. I don't even think we're close yet. Probably we're not.

We could make it back before it's dark, says the Monkey King.

We could keep an eye out for rabbits, says Lizzy. I'm getting awfully hungry.

I am, too, says Zander.

All right then, we'll do that, says the Monkey King. I'm sure we'll find something on the way.

Zander points, there's a fine lookin turtle, right there.

I make a good turtle soup, says the Monkey King.

No.

They look at Lizzy.

Why not, Lizzy? asks Zander. We have it all the time.

I know we do, and that's the problem. I don't like it, not one bit do I, and I'm sick of it.

Lizzy?

Leave that nice old turtle alone.

That's okay, says the Monkey King. We'll find something else. C'mon, we'll find a rabbit.

At the back of the brick house they climbed a black wrought iron fire escape.

She pushed open the French windows into the back of pulled sheer white curtains. She stepped inside and opened the curtains more. Have a seat.

Here?

Yes.

He sat into the window opening with his back against the one side, his feet against the other. The room was white, all of it, the bed, the lamp next to it, the vanity across from the bed, and the small carpet.

She placed her boots and jean jacket behind a white closet door and closed the door. She looked back at Finn. Would you like a glass of wine? Or a beer?

A beer would be great, thanks.

I'll be right back.

He watched her go, and when she did, he stepped back onto the fire escape and searched his pockets for a cigarette. He found half a smoked down one in his shirt pocket and lit it and looked at the surrounding houses, the few with lights on, and past them, the shaded silhouette of the town. Beyond that, the flat scrubby land where the river was and he thought of home—of Cael and Mackenzie, and how he'd see them soon.

Here you go, said Isabelle.

He turned and looked at her, his beer held out in front of her, and he paused for a moment. So beautiful. The distant soft light of the world upon her. This world now. Not a past one. He turned and reached his hand over the railing and pinched off the heater of the cigarette. He put the butt in his pocket and stepped forward and took the beer. Thanks.

Take that out of your pocket.

What?

Finn?

He took the butt out of his pocket and held it out toward her.

She laughed. I don't want it. Pitch it over the side.

L.A.?

Yup.

Sugar pushed off the stool. Baby, really? She bit her bottom lip.

Yeah, why not?

She screamed, turning around in little short tiptoe steps, her hands flapping at her sides, and now around Jared's neck. Oh my god, this is the best. You're the best. She pushed away and stood before him, naked to her dreams. I may not become a huge star, she pointed to the poster by the fridge, but I can do that. She bounced, her hands flapping again. Tell me more. When?

Not long.

She shrieked and tiptoed danced again, round and round.

California, she said.

Jake entered the drive-shed and walked to the fridge and grabbed a beer. Ya think maybe you should try again? He opened the beer and threw the cap at the garbage can.

Jared, wire brushing a motor part, looked back at Jake. Is that what ya want?

Hell, I don't know. I ran into Amanda a couple times. And her boy, too, Hunter.

How'd that go?

It was all right. She looks good. The kid seems nice enough.

Give em time.

Ha, yeah. Jake took a sip of beer. I don't think she'll stick around.

I wouldn't think so. Probably best, though, don't ya think?

I suppose. He joined Jared at the workbench and leaned against it and took a sip of beer. How's Alice?

Same, I suppose.

Ever get tired of just being here? Born and bred?

Jared walked to the fridge and grabbed a beer. He opened it and walked back to the workbench and leaned against it next to Jake. I never used to, or even thought about it much, to be honest. Not really. Not that I can remember. And now I don't know what's better, just livin and not noticing, or wondering.

Hard to say.

Wondering can lead to all sorts of trouble, said Jared. He tipped back his beer. Not wondering, I dunno, it can make ya feel kinda stupid, when ya think about it. Ya know what I mean?

Yeah. He looked at Jared. Sugar's gettin restless.

Oh?

Yeah.

'Bout what?

Jake lowered his beer. I dunno, just rattlin around here with nothin to do, I guess. It's why I thought getting her pregnant might help.

Jared tipped back his beer and looked at the poster next to the fridge. Maybe it's just the wanting itself that's the thing.

Could be. Jake looked at the poster. That's not a car. He finished his beer and put the empty on the workbench. I gotta go, I'll talk to ya later.

Yeah, said Jared, later, and he watched his brother leave. He looked back at the poster. Soon, he said. And fuck this place, and everyone in it. Not you, though, Jake, although, that is what it is, and there's not much to be done about it.

Shh.

They stop.

What?

Isidore points. See the smoke?

I see it, says Lizzy.

Should we go back? asks Zander.

Isidore looks at Lizzy and Zander. No, it's fine, c'mon.

In the darkening woods they walk next to the Monkey King. They walk past ancient silent moon trees, shaped and pointed for explicit purposes, and valid still.

It's him, says Zander.

The old man in the trilby hat is sitting on a log before a small fire, cooking up a frying pan of fish mixed with vegetables and potatoes, and it smells good. He looks up. Well well well, still lost, I see. C'mon in. He leans forward, and with a fork, he mixes up the food. He looks across the fire and says, boy, there's more plates under that big pot there and probably some extra forks. Grab em out.

Zander walks to where the plates are.

I been searching all day, and it's been exhausting, I can tell ya that much.

Who you looking for? asks Lizzy.

The old man stands and bends over and grabs the handle of the heavy frying pan with the end of his shirt. Here ya go, eat this up, and he walks around hunched over forking the food onto each of their plates.

Lizzy and Zander thank him and start to eat.

Your usual wonderful fair, says the Monkey King.

Thank you, Isidore.

You already know one another? asks Zander.

Well, indeed we do, young man, says the old man.

This is Lizzy, says the Monkey King. And that's Zander.

It's a pleasure, says the old man. Now eat up, you need your strength, marching about in these woods all day.

What's your name? asks Lizzy

Well, I don't ever remember having a name, or being told what it was.

You don't? asks Lizzy.

Nope, I don't. The first memory I have of myself is fishing on the banks of a mighty river, and I was just a small boy. Alone in the world. And I did not know my name. I did not know how I got there, or why I was there. I'd never seen another living person. Not one. So I guess that makes sense then, why would I need one? For what purpose? But there I was, and I was fishing. I was catching all kinds of fish, one after the other, and they wouldn't stop coming. He looks at Zander, and I thought, I am—fishing, it's what I called it. Words I had never spoken before, but there they were, too, for I had no one to tell me what it should be called.

The Monkey King looks at Lizzy, memorized by the telling of the story, as if she were right there with him, that little boy, his words hanging just above the low, smoky fire, his voice deep and pulling to her.

To this day, I still come upon some things I have not yet seen before, and I name them too. I often wonder, when will there be an end to it? Who's to know? And what will become of me then?

Isidore places his plate on the ground and takes his harmonica from his shirt pocket and begins to play, soft and calling, speaking with his notes to the one true story of us all—I am here.

In the garden by the woods by the river.

Finn sat in the windowsill and sipped his beer. Isabelle moved his boots and sat with him, a glass of white wine in her hand.

She was so beautiful, and he could not stop looking at her.

Have you been gone long? Isabelle asked.

Three months.

That's long enough.

Yeah, it is, and I'm a little nervous about going back, to tell you the truth.

Nervous?

A little, yeah. Her face was so open, and yet, closed, too, somehow, at least it seemed to him. Lizzy wasn't like that, hers was open all the time. Cracked wide open. So much of me went with her, he told her. And not just when she died. Long before that.

Isabelle lowered her glass of wine. I'm sorry, Finn. For all of it.

The truth of it is, it's just pain—shitty, relentless pain, and it rolls. And everything seems so closed down. Trapped by it.

She looked past Finn to the rising light. Do you think it's still all out there? What they did to him?

Finn looked too. I don't know. I suppose, all these things add up, or at least, you would hope so.

I'll never forget it.

I don't think any of us ever will

And here we are now. I would have never of thought that, would you?

No, and he looked at her—her eyes, and he thought, when Vikings plunge.

He was silent after that.

Thinking.

Thinking what?

He didn't know, standing there, this beautiful woman before him. He did know this, he had no desire to add more shit to the world. There was enough already. Too much. More than enough people willing, with their needs. Wants. Rationalizing thought, like some slow-moving chromed-up validation on a Saturday night.

Well, fuck that.

Honesty. Integrity. Show me that, because I'll tell you what, this ain't no midnight run in high boots and a mind unsettled inside of itself.

Driving city streets at night.

Why?

A cup of coffee where the miles end.

Eau Gallie, and there's a ring, and it comes—and a look, and it's here now, ringing louder, yet, in these days out of days, Sam, always, at Le Nouvel Hôtel.

This inner circle of yours, break it, or break me, because that's it, isn't it? Like a summer's sun bringing the hard face of truth to us?

Have you looked away?

Will you always?

When the talking is over, what's there? When everyone's right, what's wrong?

Love, guns, and God.

What the fuck we've become.

In America now.

Or, not. Hell, what's it matter? I'll be gone soon enough, anyway. And he thought of his kids. It's your world now. Just let me send you off, someway better. That's what I want most, I guess. Just that.

Finn?

He looked at her.

You okay?

I was just thinking—.

Yes?

Yeah, you know, how we all think we can fix everything. Work harder. Be smarter. Stronger. More resilient and more determined, and you can fix anything. But you can't. And so you work harder. Your will is great, and you become more determined. And yet, it still comes, rolling, over everything, relentless, heavy and settling again, only worse—no, not worse, not really, it's just another side of it, pulling you to it, and running through you. This pain, that rolls, and won't go away. No matter what. He looked back at Isabelle. You think you can keep the kids from it. Shelter them and protect them. That's your job. But you can't, and you don't, and you fail again. But you can't fail, not for them. And then it becomes just about them. Only them. That's what you say. And you reach out, desperate, and make more mistakes, and fail once again. And so you tell yourself, or, what you start to think is, they'd be better off without you. But what you don't know, until it's all done and gone and there's no one left standing next to you, is that through it all, you are really nothing ever more than the diminishing reality of your own thoughts of yourself. And you become that thing. And so here I am, and why I took them to my parents, and why I'm nervous about going home, which to be honest, I didn't know I was ever going to do again. But I am. I'm on a bus back there later today.

She stood and walked to her vanity. She opened a drawer and removed a long black rectangular case, ornate in its Asian design. She carried the case to the bed and sat carefully placing the case on the bedside table. She flipped open the two small brass latches. From the case she removed a long glass dream stick. She held it in both her hands. She placed it on the bed and removed a small spirit lamp and placed it on the table. She lit the lamp and pinched a small bit of opium onto the end of a long needle. She held the opium over the flame and watched it cook, rotating it slowly over the flame. When the opium was golden in its color, she picked up the pipe next to her and dropped the ball of opium into the pipe. She closed her eyes and inhaled. When she opened her eyes, she looked at Finn, and he walked to her.

She inhaled on the pipe and exhaled smoke into Finn's waiting mouth, and as the smoke trailed into him, he opened his eyes, and he heard Lizzy say, don't let go, Finn. Stay.

You didn't tell me who it is you're looking for, says Lizzy.

No, said the old man, but she's out there somewhere. She's playful, and she's a shapeshifter, and she does not know yesterday, and she does not know tomorrow, which makes it kinda tricky finding her. But I will. I'll find her again yet. You'll see. I always do.

Well I hope you do.

Thank you, I do too. She's hell on wheels when left to her own devices, that's for damn sure. He looks at Lizzy. Shouldn't you be getting to sleep?

I don't always like to sleep. And in the dark I don't so much.

Ah, I see. Well Isidore is right there. He's just catching a little sleep right now, but he won't let anything happen to you.

I know. He's my friend.

Yes. He's a good friend to have, isn't he?

Un-huh. I don't know where he came from. At first I thought I made him up, and then he became real to me, and now he is real. But that doesn't seem to matter so much. He's the best friend I ever had.

Yes, he's a good friend to have.

How long have you known him?

Forever.

That's a long time.

It doesn't seem like it.

Was that story true?

Which one?

About when you were a little boy.

It's as true as I can remember it to be.

Like, Buster, I suppose.

Buster?

Isidore.

Ah, yes, I see. I know another story.

You do?

Oh, sure, I know lots. It's about fate, would you like to hear it?

What's fate?

It's a story of a young boy. Have you heard it?

I don't know.

Well, this boy, while walking in the woods, came upon a wolf.

He did?

Yes.

What did he do?

He started to run, and he kept running until he came to a high cliff. He looked back, and although he could not see the wolf, he knew the wolf was there, and so he began to climb down a long vine to get to the bottom of the cliff. As he was climbing down, he saw a raspberry bush and stopped, and since he was hungry, he tried leaning toward it to pick some, but he couldn't reach it, and so he tried, over and over, swinging toward the raspberries, forgetting all about the wolf above him, and as he did, two mice poked their heads out of a hole in the rock and began to chew the vine. They chewed and chewed until the vine broke and the boy fell to the bottom of the cliff. He looks at Lizzy, her head on his lap, sleeping, little beautiful, Lizzy. Just remember, he says, and he puts his hand to her head, fate has no memory, and it does not know yesterday, and it does not know tomorrow. And I will find her yet. Just as she will find you. If she hasn't already.

Did you just tell that story?

The old man looks at Isidore. I did, indeed.

How's mom?

She's fine. Have you seen her?

The other day, says the Monkey King. She was young, sitting in a field of tall grass.

Ah, so she's been looking out for you.

More like these two, I would think. There was a young boy and a dog out looking for her.

Yes, he's a good one, that one. Likes to be helpful. You have your hands full I see.

They're good kids.

Yes, of course. California?

Yes, and Isidore smiled. California.

PART SIX

He said, Isabelle.

I'm right here, Finn.

And he found her again, under crisp white sheets, pulling her to him. Everything he'd been. Everything she'd been. Everything they could be together. And what a thing that was, he thought. Could he? Live a life not then. How? Was it possible?

What's the point of even thinking about it, he was on a bus later today.

But still … and he looked at her again, to her beautiful green eyes, and in that glory, he fell, a distance he did not understand, and did not know if he needed to. He reached his hand to her face. Don't let me leave, he said to her softly.

Her eyes answering.

He took her by her shoulders, pushing her back from him, just a little, just enough, to see all of her, his finger moving over her, writing words slowly over her smooth, pale skin. The softest parts of her. Her back arching to their wanting—this needing of one another, and they kissed, and they kissed more, they kissed hard, deep and longing, deep and searching, his hand finding her, and she closed her eyes, and she said, yes. And he knew then, love was a choice. Love was everything. A big moon, or not. Tidewater, and all that had been, or not.

Find a way, he thought, and have this. Let the past be the past. Let the dead bury the dead. Not you. Not her. And she brought him to her, and she would never let him go.

That's what she said.

That's what he knew.

And one day, he thought, it would be true.

True by choice.

True by fate, when we don't look away.

They walk in a wide valley meadow, Lizzy stopping. I'm sixteen now, Finn.

I know it.

Kiss me.

Sweet sixteen.

Are you goin to or not?

He closes his eyes and starts to lean toward her.

You have to make it good.

He opens his eyes.

If it's gonna be forever, a first kiss has to be special.

Lizzy, stop, I'm nervous enough already.

Oh, Finn, you can't be nervous, it might not work.

Well, I am, and you're not helping. He starts to lean toward her again, and she puts her hand to his chest.

What now?

We need to get this right, and she takes him by the hand and she brings him to the warm tall grass, the blindness of the earth welcoming them, their heads touching. He puts his hand to her face. His finger moving over her.

Just kissing now, Finn, nothin else.

Shh, Lizzy.

We got a whole lifetime of something else. Course, that's if ya can get this first kiss right, we do.

You're horrible, and he kisses her, long and deep, long and forever, and it adjoins them.

Well?

Lizzy opens her eyes and looks at Finn. We need to do it again.

He smiles, and they bring all their hopes and dreams to one another, kissing, and not stopping, until the sun starts to fall, bringing them back again.

She walked into the store.

Standing behind the counter, her husband looked up. Everything okay?

Fine.

If we needed something, why didn't you just call?

We don't need anything. She walked behind the counter and sat on the high stool next to her husband and looked at his long bony fingers taping up a little package of returned cup hooks. She brought her hand to his, like a summoning. All the reasons why.

He looked at her. It'll be all right.

She looked back at his old now, squinting, watery blue eyes, where the truth of sadness lived and could never be hidden from her. I wish I believed that.

He's coming home, and he put his free hand to hers. He said he was, and that's that.

I hope you're right.

It won't be long now, you'll see, and he'll be home.

He was talking with Zander. Isidore and Lizzy sleeping.

You're friends with Isidore?

Yes, among other things, said the old man.

He thinks we were all Black at one time. Did ya know that?

He did?

Yup.

What a strange man.

So ya don't think it's true?

Oh yes, of course, I do.

Wait. You do?

Yup.

I can see how the sun can tan you up some, but I can't see how it could turn ya'll Black.

No?

No. Besides, they're different in all sorts of ways.

Oh, how's that?

They talk different, for one thing. And how they dress and what they eat. All sorts of things, actually.

Zander, are you that snake in the grass over there looking at us?

There's a snake there?

Yup. The old man lights a cigarette and throws the wooden match to the fire. He crosses his legs and leans his elbow on his knee and takes a drag. Are you?

No, of course, not.

Well, what are you then?

I dunno, just me, I guess.

Yes, right, you see, just like that, just you, as is every other person—just them. Your past, too, it's just yours, and can't be anyone else's. But the thing with that is to remember it's past. It's gone. Don't bring it with you. It'll be there enough already. What you know—what you want from it, is never there, it's here. He takes another drag of his cigarette and exhales and points with the cigarette to the darkness. Look at this world, Zander, have a good look, it's beautiful in its offering and ruthless in its taking, and that's not always an easy thing, and so, is that not enough? Do we need more? He looks back at Zander. What is it you like to do?

I like to catch crayfish.

There you go then. Why?

I dunno, I just do.

Right. Be more of that. The more the better. He takes a last drag of his cigarette and flicks into the fire. And watch out for beliefs, they're nasty little things, like a trap that can catch you up in your own box. It's best to avoid them, if ya can, which you can. Just be Zander, and love until the end, and love now, here, in a real way, that is you. Make that enough, for it is, and always will be. Otherwise, I don't know, it makes for a sad state of being, does it not? Now, let's have a drink, there's a bottle of bourbon over there, we got some time yet, and we could use some fire in our bellies.

Zander fetches the bottle and hands it to the old man who pours some into two glasses. He hands one to Zander. There you go—to good health. And remember, Zander, in a lot of ways, we become what we see, and I can see Fate, and that's just the way that is, and I'll find her yet.

She reached her hand to his face, the sheet falling from her shoulder, the world there in its offering.

I don't want to leave.

You're on a bus back to Tidewater.

Come with me.

You know I can't. I've got my father.

I'll delay a bit. Least for a while.

You can't do that, either. Your kids are waiting for you. Don't you think they've waited long enough? And do you really want to disappoint them?

Again?

Finn.

No, I don't.

So that's it then, there's nothing that can be done about it. At least, for now. I'll get us a coffee. Black, right?

He nodded, and she got up, naked before him, and he knew, he'd never live without her.

Somehow.

But he also knew, if it wasn't that, in the here and now of the present, it wouldn't be at all. He had no room left for what wasn't actual, and before him.

Alive, and real in the world today, is what he needed.

You can keep your dead—your ghosts, if you want em, but it's not for me. I've had enough of that. More than enough.

She opened her wardrobe and took her bathrobe down from a hook on the back of the door and put it on. She looked back at Finn. I'll be right back.

He rolled onto his back, his hands behind his head, and he thought, there's a way. There has to be, and he closed his eyes and fell back to sleep.

What do you see, Hunter?

He looked up at his grandfather. Tidewater.

That's right, Tidewater. All those houses and buildings, they're a collective. Do you know what that means?

Hunter shook his head, no.

A group of like-minded people, good people, Hunter, who hold the same values close to themselves as we do, such as living a virtuous life in the name of our Lord, guided by His hand, and only His hand. But it's not always easy. He looked at Hunter, there are sacrifices that must be made, hard ones, and so we must stay strong, no matter what, even when that means doing the harder of two things, and yet, there are those that will, and often do, weaken in such moments. He placed both his hands on the boy's shoulders, and bent down before he him, looking the young boy in the eyes, and that is what we do, Hunter, we're Sterlings, we help those who may not feel His hand upon them as strongly as we do, or who tire and weaken, and it's our job to help steady them, to help keep this beautiful collective on a true path of glory. Do you understand?

Hunter nodded. Yes, sir, we're Sterlings.

That's a good boy, we're Sterlings.

Finn.

He opened his eyes and she was there, two mugs of coffee. He sat up and she handed him one. She placed hers on the nightstand and she got back into bed.

Finn sipped his coffee.

She reached for hers. What time is your bus?

Four o'clock. What time's it now?

Seven, she said.

Good. We've got more time yet.

Not really.

He looked at her. Oh?

I have some … work, I need to do shortly. But it won't take long. Can you come back? Say around ten thirty?

Yeah, of course. Now?

No. Not now. Finish your coffee.

She hadn't been out of this godforsaken town for how long? She didn't know, she couldn't remember. Stuck here. For too damn long.

Not anymore, not now, and now I have a real shot, finally, and nothing is goin to stop me.

She could stop in and see her momma on the way and let her know she was goin to California.

And Sugar wondered, was she there still?

How's long's that been?

She didn't know.

And her daddie? She hadn't thought of him—in how long? Wherever the hell he was?

What a life, smoking all the time and bitchin and cleanin sand out of the trailer, and gettin meaner all the time about everything—I coulda done somethin if it hadn't been for you slowin me up. What was I to do, left on my own like that, by that no-good spineless drinkin bastard, and don't think I didn't think about it, given you up and livin a real life for myself, cause I did, every single goddamn day, I did. I would have deserved it too.

Fuck you, is what Sugar had thought about that, and she said, I guess I still do.

Finishing up the last of the dishes, she wiped her hands on the drying towel and she walked out the side door and stood in the flat midday heat looking at the scrubby land and the few big leafy trees and the long reaching fields and beyond that— California.

She looked at Jared's house.

Alice.

She smiled.

Why didn't you tell me? How long has that been? Are they even Jared's kids? I suppose it doesn't really matter, does it?

She sat on the step and took her cigarettes from her bathrobe pocket and lit one. It's the quiet ones ya gotta watch out for. Good for you, I'm glad ya got someone, and I hope he cares for ya—and if ya wanted them kids, good for you, too, but no thank you, I ain't given up my chances. Nope, I ain't. Not now.

Not ever.

I'm goin to California, and she thought about that, and she smoked more, and she smiled. Fuck em all, she said. California.

He did what was expected, what was planned, something had to be done, his art wasn't selling, and Amanda was cut-off again.

We'll get out from under this and get ahead.

Amanda had said, yes, we'll do it, it's a good plan. Fuck him.

Yes, he said. Fuck him.

And they did.

And the Quiet Man came, once again.

Jake fished, his pickup parked, a favorite quiet spot, a beer and the river, and he thought about Sugar, and he thought about Jared, and he fished more. Being deceived like that. Being lied to and cheated on. There was only one thing he could do about it, and that was to disentangle from it, completely. There was no other self-respecting option. And once he had, that was it, love her or not, he'd put a dagger in the heart of that shit, and get himself right, in the here and now. He'd claim that, and in doing so, he'd claim himself, once again. There'd be no half-assed lingering over betrayal. No frozen moments in time idealized.

Not for him.

Why would he give either one of them the time of day of his heart? He wouldn't. He just couldn't bring himself to give them the satisfaction of that.

And Amanda? He owed her that, too, if he was honest about it.

His heart.

Otherwise, it's just filling in time that's not this time. And who needs a life lived like that?

Not him.

Not him, for goddamn sure.

He'd figure it out. Only this time, he thought, he'd think it through. Be smart about it. It wouldn't hurt, for a goddamn change.

There was a tremendous amount of people turned out and searching the woods, state troopers, too, for it had become perfectly clear the children had not runaway. They'd been taken. Abducted by a killer.

A Black one.

First Edward, then poor, Kerry. Both their children missing like that—abducted, such a horrible thing, and although they weren't perfect, not by any means, Lord knows who is, they didn't deserve this, not this, and are any of us safe now? In our own damn beds.

Who would do such a thing?

What's this world coming to?

Somethin needs to be done with … these people.

These damn people.

Sooner the better.

Lord please, guide our hand, and keep us safe, in this world built by you. For you.

Always.

Finn walked the quiet empty streets toward the town square.

He'd never been with another woman.

I think I remember her now, seeing her in the schoolyard, being teased. I'm pretty sure it was her. It's the eyes. Her mother was … from Taiwan, maybe. Something like that.

Anyway, it was her, I'm pretty sure.

He reached the Sunday Morning Café and tried the door. It was open, and he walked inside.

Drunk to hell they stagger, the soft mossy ground betraying their footing, the light tricking their way through the woods without gain and one of them saying, carry my pack, cause fuck this, and he sits down, flat-out down, surprised at his landing, his rifle across his lap, and he laughs. Fuck it.

The others, leaning against trees, squinting to the early morning sun, laugh too.

The seated man looks back, wiping the sweat from his forehead. You're out there somewheres, aren't ya, ya Black bastard?

Ya fuckin Black bastard.

And we are gonna fuck you up.

That's right, say the others.

Fuck you up bad.

Worse than that.

Worse than a fuckin dog.

And why wouldn't Finn think, it's all right, and to tell himself not to feel bad? There's not a damn thing he can do about Lizzy. Not anymore, and it's been long enough. He knows he was better off having been away, making the money that he did. Good money. It's hard being a man without money. It plays with your mind. Makes you do strange things.

The waitress appeared and he ordered his breakfast.

Jake was driving, and thinking still, and he was gettin madder than hell with every mile. With every moment lived within the confines of betrayal.

Living within the restrictions of this place.

Other people's fear, and other people's ways.

Fuck that. No kids, his wife fucking his brother, and there he was, working in that man's mill, still.

In this ruined place.

And so, why are you?

It was a good question.

And he asked himself, aren't you tired of others doing your thinking for you? Based on nothing but their money, and wanting more of it? Their greedy little get ahead clubs, and then standing up like they were better than everyone else, moralizing, telling everyone what is, and what isn't, how to live your life— and worse yet, all their damn supporters. Dirt poor and thinking they're something else; something better, just for thinking like they'd been told to, so they could feel like they're one of them. Or, at least, better than those not in the club.

It's pathetic.

I'm right and better than you for being right.

Fuck you.

My father, and his father before him, all the way back—to what? All those days best forgotten.

It's lazy, and it's useless. The very same as remembered moments born from deceit. Fear and betrayal.

There's buying and there's selling, but when it comes to your mind, there's no last refuge. Not one.

Not here.

Not anymore.

Having slowed driving past the Harvest-Wright church he pulled over to the side of the road. He looked down at his assault rifle leaning against the seat next to him, and he put his hand to it. Don't think there's not power here, too, because there is.

He looked back at the church.

A tall man in a suit was standing speaking at a podium reading a document. Sterling Spalding and several others sitting on chairs on the stage behind him. The man at the podium said, The sovereign-association of the newly formed United Christian Federation of America (UCFA) and the United States of America (USA), whereby the USFA declares itself a sovereign nation, inside of, while maintaining, a formal relationship with the nation, USA, as covered in the following constitutional framework. The man looked up. It then goes on for some 86 pages. Eighteen months of drafting. You each have a copy. Look at it, think about it, you have four hours, then we'll meet again, decide on any changes, requiring a unanimous agreement. In the meantime, no one leaves the room. You'll hand your copies in before we adjourn, and you'll pick up your phones on the way out.

Sterling stood and walked to the podium and he put his hand on the tall man's shoulder and leaned toward the mic. Everything's ready to go, it's just these final readings, and any agreed upon amendments, and that's it. All that's left. And keep in mind, two years now, nothings leaked, and we plan on keeping it that way. He started to leave and stopped and leaned back toward the mic. Humble before God.

And everyone in the room said, praise Jesus.

The meeting in the church, attended by all representatives of the one hundred and thirty seven founding counties of the United Christian Federation of America, broke up, with each man starting to read the document.

Sterling said to the tall man next to him, I'm still worried.

We met with him last night, everything's fine.

It had better be.

He's on board. This goes to the highest office, you know that. We're solid still, on all fronts. The support is overwhelming. If anything, the pressure is to open it up more.

Not yet. Let's see what we have first.

The ones that want in on the founding, they're the ones won't stop pushing.

And?

It's handled, for now.

Good. We'll talk later.

They were on their own again, just the three of them, walking in the morning of the woods, on their way to California.

Lizzy smiling, the sun breaking through the trees. Just for me, she thought. That's my sun.

I'm glad we're still going to California, says Zander. I feel better about that.

Do you? asks the Monkey King.

Yes.

And you, Lizzy?

Oh, I'm fine. I'm happy. This is a beautiful morning.

Good, says the Monkey King. And so, here we are again, on our way to California.

An older man in a suit climbed Isabelle's fire escape. He opened the French style windows and entered the room.

Isabelle in bed said, you're late.

Yeah, I know. I can't stay.

He was a hard looking man, but refined in his manner. He walked to the edge of the bed and sat down. He put his hand to Isabelle's forehead, and he moved aside a wisp of hair. I might not be back. He looked toward the window. If at all.

Oh?

He looked back at Isabelle. Trouble.

And that's new?

Not like this. He stood and walked to her vanity table. He removed something small from his pocket and looked back. I want you to hold onto this.

What is it?

Never mind. Leave it here, and he opened her jewelry box and put it there, closing the lid. Just leave it, you understand. Never move it. Don't touch it.

What's going on?

He walked to the window and looked out. He looked back at Isabelle. I can't stay. But look, I'll keep up your monthly payments, without my being here, but I need to know, he pointed to the vanity desk, that stays there. And never talk about it to anyone. Understand?

She nodded. Yeah. I understand.

In a while, I'll get in touch. We'll go from there.

All right, she said, and she wondered, was she really free of this man, just like that? After all of this time?

She hoped so, and she thought of Finn.

I gotta go, the man said, and he stepped back out the fire escape and walked down the stairs.

PART SEVEN

She screamed, he's dead.

Who's dead?

You evil fucking man. I hate you. Beyond hate. Do you know that? And despite her rage, everything around her—all the sounds around Amanda, slowed. Her father's breathing. Her accelerated heart. The crushing silence of knowing she was defeated.

Once again.

That she'd lost.

Looking for these?

Regaining her focus, she looked at her father holding her car keys. There's always death around you. Do you know that? No matter what. No matter when.

Is that right? Well, there's not a chance in hell I'd let you take him. He moved toward his daughter. You honestly thought, you and your boyfriend, in his limited abilities, and your lack of understanding of the world, could pull such a thing off? Why?

Why what?

He was standing before her. Why be my enemy? All these years? You want to blame me for your mother and your brother?

You go right ahead, but I have done nothing but try and make our world a better place, including for them, and you. And yet, you fight me still. Your anger blinding you to the realities of this world. Well, not me.

Go to fucking hell, and she reached forward. Give me those.

He stepped back, putting the keys in his pocket.

His phone in his hand now, he hit the Quiet Man on speed dial. He put the phone to his ear, and said simply, it's time.

Finn had been done breakfast for a while. He'd worked through several coffees and cigarettes. He looked at the clock on the wall. It was ten. He looked at the bill on the table, and he reached into his pocket and took out his money and dropped some bills down. He stood and walked to the door.

Thank you, the waitress called out. Have a good day.

Finn looked back. Thank you. You too.

Standing on the sidewalk boards, he looked around. The small town had started to wake up.

What there was of it.

Walking, he heard Lizzy's voice in the blinds of the edges of the sun reaching him. Isn't she the most beautiful baby ever born?

Yes.

We'll have another one, a boy.

We will?

Yes, of course, we will. But it was important to have this girl, first. Don't ya think? Hold her, Finn, feel the meaning of us. Take her in your arms.

And he remembered that he did, everything else falling away. And now, his kids were waiting for him—had been, for too long, and he couldn't let them down. But he also knew, he didn't want to leave her. To be without her.

Isabelle.

And yet, he thought, who was she? Did he really know her? Was she what he thought she was. Is anybody?

He didn't know, and he started on his way back to her.

Tidewater Psychiatric Hospital and Hope House.

It's where Amanda was now, and would be, for a very long time.

The Quiet Man had entered the house, followed by a doctor and two large medical attendants. They sedated her and removed her from the house in a wheelchair, but not before taking her phone.

The Quiet Man stayed behind, taking care of the details, and telling the staff, she had gone back home. He packed up all of her things and loaded them into her car and he drove the car away.

She was placed on a 72 hour hold.

All that was required?

The signature of one psychiatrist.

Next would come a thirty-day hold. Again, one signature. Beyond that, they'd appear before a judge and state their case, all the reasons—all the documentation necessary, to show why Amanda Sterling was a danger to herself, and society, and should not be freed from their care. The two lawyers and the judge in agreement, long before the case would ever be heard.

Sterling would see to it.

Her rights, and her freedom, gone.

And Sterling Spalding smiling, thought, enough entitlement, enough being on the wrong side of right. He was done with those battles. He didn't have the energy, or the time. Not anymore.

She would never have changed, and taken the boy with her, and made a mess of that, and he just couldn't let that happen. It was too important, this lineage. A lineage he felt a responsibility to nurture and keep in place. The continuation of Sterlings, and their place in the world. He had worked too hard, his entire life, to achieve what he had. Things that had to be continued, no matter what, at all cost.

What then was he supposed to do?

She'd be moved from the hospital portion of the building to Hope House, an exclusive, and difficult place to be admitted to. One had to be rich, white, and unwanted. Amanda Spalding was all of those things.

Sterling was on the board, and the largest donor. It wasn't difficult.

Hunter, of course, would be placed under his legal guardianship. He might even adopt the boy. He'd have to see about that.

Marisa was in the kitchen with the boy, making him lunch. She had turned and looked in the direction of the sound of Amanda's car pulling away. She wasn't sure what to do? Even though, she knew it was best to do nothing. She looked back at the boy. Best for her, she thought. I'm not so sure about you, or your mother. Eat your lunch, she said. That's a good boy.

Jake opened the door and walked to the fridge. He took out a beer, opened it, and tipped it back. He leaned against the fridge. Ever feel like not being here?

Jared looked back. What day is it?

Wednesday.

Then, yup.

Jake laughed. Ain't that the fuckin truth of it.

Everythin all right?

I suppose. He tipped back his beer. I wouldn't worry about helping me out with Sugar no more.

No?

No. To be honest, she seems to be against the idea.

Things'll work out.

Will they?

Jared walked to the fridge and grabbed a beer. He sat on one of the blocks of cracked white oak and opened the beer.

Jake joined him. Remember that time when mom was alive and she wanted us to see the North?

Yeah, sure. We went and saw the cracked bell.

Right.

What about it?

Ever think about going back up there?

Where? North?

Yeah.

No, why?

I don't know. Get the fuck out of here, I guess.

Jared looked at his brother. Well, that I can understand. I just couldn't see goin back up there again. No reason to.

No, I suppose not. But I'll tell you what, I sure as fuck am tired of having my life run for me. Especially by the ways of people down here.

Jared took another sip of beer. I wonder sometimes, if one place is ever better than the next? Or just different, maybe?

Jake finished his beer, stood and threw the empty at the garbage can. That could be right. I suppose it is. But one thing's certain, better or not, it ain't fuckin here.

True enough. Jared stood. Everything seems a little different, lately, don't it?

Well, I don't know if it's any different, or were just seeing it differently?

That could be it.

I think it's more than just could be. I gotta go.

Jared watched Jake walk to the door, and he said, later. Or, perhaps, not, he thought. As sad as that might make him. And he knew it would—but whatever. What had to be done, had to be done, and that was that.

Yeah, said Jake, later, and he walked out the door.

They'd passed out from their all-night into the next day drinking. One man woke, squinting his eyes to the hard sun above him. He thought he heard a sound. He listened more, and it was there again, the distant sounds of someone walking in the woods. He elbowed the man next to him. Wake the fuck up. He checked his rifle and switched the safety off.

What? said the other man.

There's someone out there.

You sure?

Yeah, I'm sure. He stood, listening more. Hear that?

No, I don't hear a damn thing.

Get up, and get the others up too. I'm tellin ya, there's somethin out there.

The old man with the trilby hat was rowing a small boat across a small lake. He was talking, as if there was someone in the boat with him. The sky, a brilliant blue, no clouds, a small breeze. My only point is this, it's become tedious. Tiresome, tedious, and predictable. These times of transition, they always make me anxious. He rowed more. Although, it's one of my favorite parts, of the things these people do. New gods with new stories, and who the keeper of these stories will be? What they'll be like, these new ones not to be trusted. Soon, my lovely, not long now. Just the blink of an eye, really. Less, perhaps. One or two hundred years. No more. No time at all. My goodness me, isn't it just all so wonderful? He put up the oars and let the boat drift. Lighting a cigarette, he leaned back, looking to the wide-open blue sky. He exhaled. All the world before him.

Fuck it, he called in sick. He couldn't do it. More lost time. More time taken from him just to empower the sick fucked life of a man on top of a hill.

It'll tumble, he thought. It can't hold.

And just maybe I can help it. Do something useful for a change.

Something with meaning.

He drove the streets of Tidewater, looking at all the lost, daytime souls. Some sitting, Some walking, Some standing.

He saw a man and two women, both women carrying bibles.

There's no coming back. Not now.

It's gone too far.

He made it to the top of the hill, parked, and stepped out of the truck.

Marisa was straightening Amanda's room. Changing the bedding. A warm breeze pushing in the opened French doors, and she walked to them, and saw him there, standing at the edge of the hill looking up. Amanda's man, Burelson.

Go to him, she thought.

Help Amanda.

Help the boy.

Finn was taking his time walking back to Isabelle's place. He was early. He stopped and looked at the town square and the bench there. He looked around and he wondered, where's that old man? The one with the shopping cart and the squeaky wheel?

Here, right here, and he tipped his trilby hat back, pulling on a cigarette, leaning against a brick wall.

Finn, seeing the old man, smiled.

Lizzy, what do you think of all of this? It's all a bit crazy, isn't it? This life.

This world.

Or is it just me? Have I lost my mind, finally.

Perhaps, it is that, he thought, and he walked on.

How is one to know?

Well?

Well, what?

Did he say anything?

Jared wiped his hands and threw the rag on the workbench and turned and faced Sugar. Yeah, but not too much.

And?

And, what?

Jesus Christ. She walked to the fridge and opened a beer. She took a sip. He knows.

What'ya mean, he knows?

What don't ya understand about that?

About us? Jared walked past Sugar and grabbed a beer. How do ya know that?

I know, because we got in a fight last night, that's how.

What'd he say?

Said he was done livin lies. Or, as he put it, fuckin lies.

Yeah, he's been in a mood, that's for damn sure.

A mood? Are you kiddin me? I've never seen him like this. Said he was done with it all. And when I asked him what he meant by that, he just said, what it means. Said, he didn't give a shit what I did, as long as I was happy. Now, isn't that the very worst thing a person could say? Trying to make me feel guilty for his neglect and his small town thinking. She started to pace, back and forth in her flip-flops, drinking her beer. Like I didn't try, all those years.

He said that?

She stopped and looked at Jared. What?

That he didn't care what you did, as long as you were happy?

Oh, he knows how to dig the knife in, that's for damn sure.

Well, isn't that a good thing then? And what makes you think he knows about us?

Dear God help me.

What?

Are you dumb?

Look, Sugar, I don't fuckin know, all right.

Know what?

What the hell it is you're talkin about. How does he know about us?

Why else would he say he didn't care what I did? Why else would he suddenly not care about having kids?

That's all he said? He didn't say it directly, that he knew about us?

What? You need to be hit over the head with it? He knows. And don't think I don't know it has to do with that Amanda Sterling, because I do. I know what she's meant to him.

So what? Suddenly you care how he feels? I thought you'd be happy?

She pulled herself up onto the stool, crossed her legs, and took a sip. It's just irritating, that's all. Of course, I'm happy. That is, if we're really still going?

Jared looked out the window at his brother's place.

Well? Are we?

He looked back at Sugar. Did he say anything else?

Nope. But he was angry, that's for damn sure. I don't know what he's up to, but he's up to something. He took that gun with him. The one I won't let em keep in the house.

The AK?

Why would I know what you call it? But it ain't there now.

Jared looked back out the window, and he said, Jake. Jesus fuckin Christ.

She's not here, said Marisa. She had approached him, standing where he always did, at the edge of the property, where the ground started to slope down. The town below them.

What do you mean, she's not here? What about the boy?

She looked around. They took her.

Took her? Who?

A doctor and two other men. In a wheelchair. Hunter is still here.

To the hospital? Is she okay?

It wasn't the hospital. Not the main one.

What?

Hope House, Mr. Burelson.

Fuck me. Was she okay?

I don't know. I was told to watch Hunter. In the kitchen.

Her car's gone.

They took it, and all her things too. They told me she went back home to New York and Hunter was staying with us.

He looked at the house, and then back at Marisa. Thanks.

Standing at his study window, Sterling watched Jake turn and walk back down the slope of the hill. He reached into his pocket and took out his phone. We need security here, he said to the Quiet Man. I'm worried about the boy. Send over a dozen Oath Holders. We might have some trouble. Make it you're very best men.

A small stream next to a field of tall grass, a slight breeze picking up, and now, standing in the middle of the field, a woman. Tall and beautiful. Long fair hair. And she is raging, for you can see it, she has storms in her eyes.

Lizzy stopping, looking at the field.

Isidore stops and looks at Lizzy, at her freckles, scattered over her small, button nose. Her eyes, wide and innocent, trusting, and yet, showing the betrayal of trust too. He puts his hand to the baldness of his head, and he asks her, do you see her?

Lizzy nods. She looks at Isidore. Who is she?

Isidore looks back at the field. I think she's looking out for us. What do you think?

I think so too. Look, and Lizzy points. The boy and that dog, the one that looks like a wolf.

Yes.

Ty.

Yes.

Don't fuckin move.

The six men, their guns drawn.

Jesus Christ, says one. Would you look at the size of em.

Fuck me, says another.

Nigger, don't even think 'bout movin, or we will take you down.

Abducting them children like that.

He didn't do anything, says Zander. Leave us alone.

Murderin fuckin bastard.

Lizzy looks back to the field. The woman is no longer there. The young boy and the dog are not there. Ty, she whispers.

Isidore reaches his hands out and moves the children behind him. You don't need those guns, we'll come with you.

Fuckin right you'll come with us.

On your fuckin knees.

And the Monkey King does, taking a rifle butt to the head.

Two of the men reach out and grab the children, the children screaming, the men forcing them back to the truck. Their crying, and they scream, Isidore. Buster. No, please. Someone, help us, please. Isidore.

The other men now, set upon him. The butts of their weapons to his head. His face. His body. Their boots. Their fists. Over and over—and more, and more yet, for all the ages. Their anger pushed on by his bringing them their fears; their hate. Ruthless, and with a vengeance. And yet, he does not fall. Swaying, back and forth with every blow. The children screaming more. Crying more. Stop stop stop. And this man's blood, it runs, to the darkening sky, to the damp blind earth, over their boots, warm and slow from their forever hands, of just like this, and always will be. The sound of the children's screaming, as if coming from everywhere, suddenly, and deafening. And they beat him, and they beat him more. And still, he does not fall.

Please, the children scream.

Every blow, for all of our time.

No, they scream.

Our Father. Our Son. Our sins.

No no no, please.

The Monkey King's blood soaking the dry, dying earth.

And don't think it won't always be like this.

Cause it will, says one of the men, and he pulls out his hunting knife, and he begins to carve up the giant man's face, on his knees before them. A Black face. A large man with a Black face. His blood running still.

That's enough. They want him alive.

Is he breathing?

Fuck me.

How we ever gonna get em out of here?

Get the truck.

And they chain him, dragging him out of the woods behind the truck.

Like a dog.

Worse than a fuckin dog.

And she is there, once again, standing in the field, this woman, Fate, with tears in her eyes.

Tears that fall for these men.

Tears that will always fall for these men.

A great sadness.

A sadness for all of our time, and time yet to come.

PART EIGHT

It wasn't a place he'd grown up knowing. He'd come attached to it all the same. The light of a harsher reality. Or, at least, one not so hidden, as if everything was before him. A quietness in an emptiness without a past. Less history. Less people having occupied it through time, and somehow, that made a difference. Made it easier to connect to it. At least, it did for him. Like the sunsets, he thought. Where he was from, they were big, too, but in a take everything away with it sort of way. As if each one embodied all of time. Here, they were just big, but only in the here and now. Only that particular moment, mattering. In a way, it made it harder to disappear here. To be less visible.

Finn was close to reaching her place, and he wondered, what good would come of it? He was on a bus later today. But he also knew, he couldn't not have her back in his arms again.

The good feel of her. As if made for him.

Figure it out, he thought, and he walked on.

Sugar knocked on the side screen door. Alice?

She heard Alice yell, c'mon in, I'm running late for work.

Jared had gone into town to get some parts for something or other. Jake, who the fuck knew? Sugar opened the screen door and stepped inside. This won't take long.

Fine, said Alice. What is it?

You're not going to like it, but here goes anyway. And the only reason I'm tellin ya, is cause I don't think he will. And I think you should know.

Alice appeared in the room wearing a white bathrobe, a white towel on her head. She had been doing her makeup. Sugar, you really want to do this now? Is it necessary?

I think it is, yeah.

If it's about you and my husband, you can save your breath.

I figured you knew.

There's little that stays a secret in this place long, is there?

No, I guess that's true. Which is why, I suppose, he knows about you and Sam down at work. I told him he should talk to you about it, but, of course, he wouldn't. He's such a Burelson.

Alice stood still, and did not say anything.

But that's not why I'm here.

No?

No. I wanted to let you know we're leaving. Soon.

Is that right?

Yup, it's right. We're goin to California.

Well, that just makes everything a little easier, doesn't it?

Oh? You were leaving him? Divorce?

That's between us.

Fair enough. Sugar looked at the two small kids in the living room area watching a TV show. He doesn't think they're his.

That's what he said. Anyway, Alice, I just wanted you to know. You've been a decent enough sister-in-law to me.

I'd like to say the same thing, Sugar.

That's all right, that's just the way it goes sometimes. Sugar looked at the kids again. Good luck, Alice, and she turned and opened the screen door and walked home.

Good luck to you, too, Sugar, said Alice. You'll need it.

Jake stopped at the gated entrance to the Tidewater Psychiatric Hospital and Hope House. The gate was open and he drove up the long, tree-lined driveway.

He drove the circle and stopped in front of the entrance. He looked at the AK next to him.

Freedom. It's what they all wanted, in their own way. Sterling. Finn. Sugar. Jake. All of them reaching to it. Reaching beyond what was right in front of them. Every lost soul of this town, too, reaching beyond what was right in front of them. Reaching to God. Just not the one walking among them. Blinded by their hate; their fear, and more of it coming.

Behind the truck, they drag him, the Monkey King man, down dirt roads, bloodied and nearly dead. A tragic silhouette to the harsh reality of us. Our minds. Our ways. But what they didn't know, was that, in their fear, they could not reach him. Only Lizzy had done that, in her ability to love without fear. Present and honest. Not in the past. Not in the future. Here, now, and without fear. Without, what could have been. What will be.

Her, love under a big moon, now, and she looked to the sky, her eyes filled with the tears of why?

Why her father?

Why these men?

Next to a long flowing river.

Tidewater, USA.

Today. Yesterday. Tomorrow.

You did what?

I talked to her. I told her. I thought she deserved at least that.

Did ya now? Well, I wish you hadn't.

No? Why? There's nothing she can do about it.

Jared looked out the window at Jake's place. He hadn't gone to get a part, he'd gone to look for Jake. He wasn't at work. He'd called in. He asked everyone in town who he thought might know. None did and he was worried, although, he tried not to be. He looked back at Sugar. No, I guess that's right.

Well, you'll be glad to know, when I said you were worried them kids weren't yours, she didn't bat an eye. Like she didn't care.

Yeah?

Yeah.

Fuck her.

That's right, baby, fuck her. We're goin, and that's all that matters. Ain't that right?

He walked to her, and she put her arms around him, and she looked up to his eyes to see the truth of it. And it was there. They really were going.

We got time, yet, she said.

Do we now, and he lifted her up onto the high stool.

She leaned back onto her elbows, his hands moving up her legs. Yes, baby, she said, and she looked out the small window to her place, and she thought, fuck you, Jake Burelson. You ain't the only one looking for what you want. But I don't think she's worth it. That's what I think.

The small fan started up, pushing warm sticky air over her, and she looked back at Jared, and she took him into her. Owning that, too, and it made her feel good. It made her feel powerful, and she'd use that power, and she'd use it right. No matter what. It was what she had, and she'd make sure it was enough.

She looked back out the small window. No small birds there.

No small birds coming.

Not this day.

Not any day now beyond this day.

And yet, there was a sadness there, much like this place itself, and no matter what she thought, or what she said, it stayed, digging its way into her very way of being, never taking away her pain in the night beneath a big moon that knows only the purity of love, and the honesty of it, and not the tricks of the mind. Whether we think we are getting away with it, or not.

And we're not.

Never have been.

Never will.

This story of Isidore. Of Lizzy.

This story of the truth of us, there and waiting.

Always.

The old man pulled the small boat up onto the far shore of the small lake. He stood looking back at Tidewater, in this time of transition, with the worst of it still to come. There's no mistaking it, he thought. There never is. If only they would realize, one day, everything they don't know, is here already. And everything they do know, never was. He looked around. And now, my dear, where are you? For real love requires no explanation. The consequences of dishonesty found in the strand of a single hair left behind.

This sadness of you.

Of never being enough, and always looking elsewhere.

In God we trust.

At the Tidewater Psychiatric Hospital and Hope House, it really was this simple: Jake checked the AK, opened the truck door, and walked through the main doors, and said, Randy?

Jake?

Yup.

The security guard looked at the AK hanging to Jake's side. What the fuck?

It's all right, just stand up.

What are ya doin, Jake?

Sterling brought Amanda in. I'm here to get her.

He nodded to the gun. Like that?

Yup, just like that. It's the only way. You have a cell on ya?

Yeah.

Take it out and put it on the ground. Oh, and the walkie.

He waited.

All right, Randy, good. Let's go check in, and get this done.

Finn stopped and looked at Isabelle's place. A light on. It was just past 10:30, and he wanted to spend all the time he could with her, before he had to go. He crossed the street and he walked down the laneway next to her house and he stopped at the base of the fire escape. He looked up at her window, and he started to climb the stairs.

Two men, climbing out of the window, started down the stairs.

Looking up, Finn stopped.

The men stop. Who the fuck are you? said the first man, and he grabbed the railings with his hands, and kicked Finn in the chest, Finn tumbling down the stairs to the laneway.

Both men, standing over Finn.

The second man, his gun out. Who the fuck is he?

No idea, replied the first man.

Yeah, well, fuck this, and the second man shot Finn in the back of the head.

The first man, looked around, and said, we can't leave him here.

No, yeah, throw him in the trunk, and let's get the fuck out of here.

Isabelle's room was ransacked, and she was beaten. She was bloodied. She was stretched out on the bed and she was only just breathing. Her father, at the doorway to her room, shot in the chest, fallen to the floor, his blood, running from him, and pooling next to him.

Sugar walked through the house in just her bathrobe, two suitcases open on her bed. She walked out the side door and stood on the little wooden stair landing. She lit a cigarette and looked at Jared's house. She looked at the slow rolling ploughed field across the road from them. The one large tree in the center of it. It's about time, she thought, and she smoked more. Imagine being stuck here. But not anymore, and that's all that matters. She took a drag and tilted her head and exhaled, and she thought of all the people she'd meet. The possibilities. She smiled, and she took another drag, and she flicked the cigarette over the railing onto the gravel driveway. It'll be like none of this ever existed.

That's the hope, and that's the wish, these possibilities of never having been.

Beautiful visions.

She walked back inside and began to pack. She was going to California.

It was happening, and it was happening for real, and out there, under the forever blue skies of California, she'd become a new version of herself.

A better version.

Beautiful and true and better.

Sterling ran the trains, naked, in the darkened room, a cigar between his fingers, a glass of whiskey.

Look at em go. Shiny and go. Round and round.

And all the world fell.

Their world. Not ours. He drank more and he smoked more in the only world that mattered now. His and God's world, as if one. For it was, he thought. Of course, it was.

He smiled, and he stood, the cigar in his mouth.

By design, and as it should be.

He took the cigar from his mouth, and he looked up, and he reached up, and he said, ego sum deus meum.

Naked. Naked to the world, the trains running on.

Look at em go. Shiny and go. Round and round.

Owned and paid for, this world. All of it. Just as it always has been, and always will be.

Beautiful visions.

Naked before God.

Finn's mother sat on the porch, her husband sleeping, and she listened to the quiet of the South. And she knew, there was something wrong, for it was there, in the deep, quiet spaces of her.

And it made her sad.

It made her cry.

More silent tears spilt in a land built upon them. Quiet, sad, and so very horrible. This impossible bliss. This—hold on, before it all breaks apart. Which, she thought, was coming one day soon. Far, too, soon, and maybe not soon enough. And she said, Lord, please watch over my boy.

Finn.

A bullet in his head.

Jake and the security guard stood at the Hope House check-in desk. You can come out from behind there, and join us, Jake said to the woman sitting behind the desk.

The woman, seeing the AK hanging from Jake's shoulder, didn't know what to say, or do, and she remained as she was. Puzzled. Stunned.

Now, Jake said. Get over here.

She got up and walked around the desk and stood in the hallway with them.

I need your phone.

The woman took her cell phone from her pocket, and she held it out to him.

I don't want it. Put it on the ground.

She did.

Take me to Amanda Sterling.

Amanda Sterling?

Yes.

The woman looked at the security guard, who nodded. She looked back at Jake. She's in room 110.

Buzz us in. I don't want any trouble. I'm just here for Amanda, and that's it. All right?

The woman nodded.

Okay then, let's go.

The woman used her security pass to open the double doors to the ward.

There were several police cars, two ambulances, and a fire truck, all parked on the road in front of Isabelle's house.

Her father dead.

Isabelle, still breathing, was wheeled into an ambulance.

The unpredictability of being, and always set into motion.

Somewhere.

Somehow.

The two men stopped at the side of the road and removed Finn from the trunk.

Just leave em, and let's go.

Wait, said the second man, and he took his gun out and wrapped Finn's hand around it, and placed it on the road.

All right, then, said the first man, let's get the fuck out of here.

Have you seen, Jake?

Nope, no one has, said Jared. I've asked around.

Well, isn't that just like him.

What?

Not to be here, when I'm finally gettin the hell out of this place.

What's it matter?

Sugar turned on the high metal stool and looked at Jared leaning against the workbench. It would have been nice, that's all.

What?

To look em in the eye when I told him, I was leaving—with you.

Jared looked at Sugar. Probably, it's okay, that you don't. I mean, do you really need that? Does he?

It would have been nice, that's all. I've earned that satisfaction. That's what I think.

Well, whatever. We're going, and that's it.

Yeah, we are. California.

Yes, Jared said, and he leaned down and kissed Sugar. Fucking right, California. Tonight.

Yes, baby, tonight, and she pulled him to her more, and kissed him again.

Lizzy, says Finn, we have to find our way back home. We have to.

We will, Lizzy. We were walking this way, remember?

I think so, but I'm not sure. Why didn't we take the usual way?

I don't know, says Finn.

Me either, says Lizzy.

It's all right, we'll get there.

I know we will. Even if it takes a little longer, right? That's okay?

Yes, Lizzy, it's okay.

It's a nice day.

Yes, it is. Do you remember that first time we walked in the woods?

Lizzy stops and looks at Finn and smiles. Yes, I remember. It was dark by the time we made it back. Your mom was so worried, and it was then I knew she loved me too.

Why, because she was worried?

Sort of.

Well, what do you mean, then?

She told me.

She told you what?

That she was worried because she loved me too, just like you. The very same.

She did.

Yes.

My dad too.

Yes, your dad too.

Finn opened his eyes, unsure of where he was, and wondering why he had a mouth full of gravel. Wondering why his head felt like it had been hit by a baseball bat, and then he remembered, he'd been kicked down the stairs. Isabelle, he said, and he tried to lift his head. He put his hand to the back of his head and felt the warm blood there. Fuck, he said. He thought of his kids, and how he had to make it back home. He couldn't let them down, not again. He closed his eyes, and said, Lizzy, help me back to them, please.

And there was no answer.

She did not reach out, and she did not touch him, and she did not say, it's okay, Finn, we can do it. We can make it back home.

Not then, not this day, not ever again.

Jake, the security guard, and the receptionist moved down the hallway. They met a doctor walking toward them. He stopped. They stopped. Jake stepped forward. It's fine. Where's your phone?

The doctor reached into his pocket and removed his phone.

Put it on the ground.

Jake waited. Now get over here.

The doctor hesitated.

Jake stepped forward, lifting the gun, and the doctor walked forward, joining them.

They moved back down the hallway, and they came to another hallway adjoining theirs. A patient, a tall, middle-aged man with disheveled grey hair, wearing a hospital gown and slippers, looked up and said, oh. He put his hand to his mouth and he said it again, oh.

Jake looked at the receptionist. Is he okay? Can he join us?

Yes, he's fine. Andrew, she said, come join us.

The man smiled, he was happy, and he walked forward and joined the others. Where?

An outing, replied the receptionist.

Oh yes, good. An outing. Okay, yes.

Does he have a phone?

No. They're not allowed to.

And who's this?

A small man standing before Jake was looking up at him. He wore a colorful sweater and a floppy hat, and he said, squeeze me.

Pierre, said the receptionist, come and join us.

Where? A concert?

Yes, a concert.

Okay, said Pierre. Good good, yes, and he joined the others.

He said to the doctor standing before him, don't ever leave me.

The doctor said, Pierre, quiet.

Yes, quiet, said Pierre, and he put his finger to his mouth. Shh, nice and quiet. Are we going to a bay in the north? Because I've had a girl there.

Jake looked back at the receptionist. Can you shut him up?

The receptionist said to Pierre, Pierre, quiet.

Yes, said Pierre, quiet. We mustn't disturb the others. In a bay. In the north. I've had a girl there.

Pierre, quiet, said the receptionist, once again.

At the side of the road, Finn could no longer lift his head from the gravel. His eyes open, watching a long line of RVs driving by, and he wondered, where were they going?
Shouldn't I be going there too? he thought.
He didn't know, but he felt like he should.
He looked at the blood on his fingers, and he said, Jesus fucking Christ.
He said, no, not yet, Please, not yet.
My kids.
He closed his eyes, the blood from his head pooling on the gravel next to him, and he said, Isabelle.

Finn's dad looked at his wife, and he knew. A lifetime. That's what he saw there. All he needed to see, and he reached out and touched her face, all of it just means this, he said to her, and he leaned forward and kissed her.
She rested her head on his shoulder, taking in the years between them. Long and silent, like the long quiet night before them, and she whispered to him, are you like me, and can't sleep?
Yes, he said.
And by the light of the moon breaking through their bedroom window, neither one spoke again, listening instead, to what the world was trying to tell them—Finn wasn't coming back. Not then. Not tomorrow.
Not ever.

Sugar's bags were on the small side door stair landing, where she sat smoking. Don't leave me sitting here, Jared Burelson. We have plans. We have dreams. And it's time now to see em through, and so, don't you dare leave me here.

Not now.

Not tonight.

It's not like there are endless opportunities. They don't last forever. We can't watch them all go by. At a certain point, we have to act. To have that courage. And we have ours, don't we? We can do it, I know we can, isn't that right? Baby, please, don't leave me here waiting like this.

Baby, please.

Perhaps still, perhaps always, in Tidewater, is the sight of a young girl sitting next to a jail wall, below a barred window, alone, broken and wondering, hoping for a better day; a better ending, that will never come.

Will it?

Can they not see her, not knowing, not understanding, but loving still? Boundless and honest in her trusting.

Trusting in her faith in love.

In her faith in us.

When she has no reason to.

Isidore, bloodied and nearly dead, stretched out on the floor of a locked cell.

Sterling, with the guards of their Lord patrolling the grounds, stood next to the Quiet Man, looking down at Tidewater. It took the alignment of so much unseen, for this to happen. Which can only be viewed as the hand of Him, and His consent.

His and ours, said the Quiet Man.

Sterling looked at the Quiet Man. Yes. He looked back at Tidewater stretching out before him. The long winding river. And yet, without the blessings of this administration—of the American people themselves, it couldn't of happened. We are truly blessed, to be standing on the edge of history. This history, Returning, as we are, to what once made us great. And will again.

And so it will be, just that, said the Quiet Man. By the hand of Him, and us.

We are humbled before God, we truly are.

Yes, we are.

It's time now.

Praise Jesus, said the Quiet Man.

Amen, said Sterling, and he looked back to Tidewater.

His town, he thought.

His way.

His and God's way.

In the hospital, Isabelle was unconscious for several days, and when she woke, she said, Finn. Oh god, Finn. I am so sorry.

Finn.

By the time they reached room 110, there were eight or nine people accompanying Jake, a trail of cell phones on the floor behind them.

This is it? asked Jake.

Yes, Randy said.

Open the door.

The security guard stepped forward and unlocked the door.

There was an anti-room, with another security guard, sleeping in a chair. He woke. What the fuck?

It's all right, said Randy.

Give me your cell phone and your walkie, said Jake.

He did, and Jake dropped them to the floor. He looked back. Everyone squeeze inside.

When they had, Jake looked at the new security guard, and said, open the door.

The man looked at Randy, who nodded, and he stood, and unlocked the door.

Jake looked back. No one move. Just stay where you are. This'll only take a minute. Randy, give me a hand, and together they moved toward Amanda, medicated and sleeping on a bed, her arms and legs bound in restraints.

God slept.

Under a big tree. His trilby hat tipped forward.

And Fate? She never slept, always there, with us. And this day? With the wind, carrying our thoughts to her. Our thoughts of time. Our thoughts of us in time.

Saying, come.

Come, see what we have become.

In this garden, coming.

Jared pulled the truck up and stopped, and Sugar stood and said, are you kidding me?

The moon there, large and hanging over the river, waiting too. Watching. Watching everything.

Watching us.

He got out and walked around the truck and grabbed Sugar's bags. Sorry. Some things took a little longer than I thought. But we're good now.

Sugar opened the passenger door and got in. Whatever. Let's just go. I can't wait another minute. My god, finally.

Jared walked back around the truck and got in. He looked at Sugar. Ready?

Ready? I've never been more ready for anything in my entire life. She leaned forward and kissed him. I can't believe we're actually doing it. Thank you, baby. A new start to a new life.

Jared dropped the truck in gear and headed back down the gravel driveway. At the road he turned left. After a while, he took another left, and drove up a long straight road.

At the top of a high hill, he stopped the truck and looked back.

What? said Sugar.

When he didn't answer, and stayed looking behind him, Sugar looked too. And in the distance, in this night of their beautiful vision, Jared's house exploded, breaking into flames, that reached far into the night.

Sugar's hand came to her mouth. She looked at Jared. Were they?

He looked at Sugar, his eyes telling her everything she needed to know.

Oh God, she thought, those poor children. This place, and she looked down the road stretching out before them. She leaned against the car door, feeling cold, and feeling alone, and she said, California.

He dropped the truck back into gear and he drove into the night of their new life, waiting. Yes, baby, he said, California

And Zander? He was never the same.

All those nights of climbing, and never leaving, this pushing back of his not becoming that.

In the heat of every night.

The confirmation of his conditioning. His un-choosing.

His fear, brought to him.

He never settled, always moving. One place, the next place, all of them the same in their disguises of what they really were, running electric just below his skin. A raging against what he would not be, no matter what, and yet, climbing—climbing always, into the arms of yesterday, still.

And now dead. Just a young man, and now dead.

One escape—one mainline, too many.

They had held a gun to her head, and when she wouldn't tell them where it was—that which they had come for, they beat her, and they beat her until she did tell them.

And yet, where was Finn? Why hadn't it been him that found her? She didn't know, and she was worried. Had he gone back to Tidewater? She'd be released soon, and when she was, she'd find him. And nothing, she thought, will keep her from finding him, for there was nothing keeping her here now, either.

Only freedom, of a certain type.

The kind you can't escape.

His heart was racing.

He could feel it.

He needed to get back to his kids.

How?

He didn't know, but he needed to. He absolutely had to. Somehow.

Someway.

He closed his eyes again, and he did not say Isabelle, and he did not say Lizzy, for there was only the heart of darkness there, at the side of a road, beneath the fading light of a falling midnight sun.

Freed from her restraints, Randy and Jake settled Amanda into a wheelchair.

Give me your keys.

Jake took the keys from Randy and turned to the group of people. I'm goin to lock in here. It won't be long until someone comes and lets you out, but I need a head start. Is that fair? Y'all okay with that?

The group gave their consent, most of them nodding, and he wheeled Amanda out of the room, stopping, locking the door behind him.

He pushed her back down the hallway, and out the main doors.

At his pickup, he lifted her from the wheelchair, and placed her in the truck.

He walked around the truck, placed the AK in the back, and got in and drove away.

He drove through the night, the whole of the night, until arriving, with the sun rising, at a small abandoned cabin that had been in his mom's family for over one hundred and eighty years. He hadn't been there since he and Jared were kids.

Amanda woke, watching Jake forcing open the front door.

He walked back to the truck. We're here now, he told her.

Where? she asked.

Somewhere far, where we won't be found.

He has Hunter still, doesn't he?

Yes, Jake said. He does.

She closed her eyes, and she cried.

He helped her down from the truck, and together, they walked into the cabin, and closed the door.

The reality of Tidewater, like an undercurrent of a quiet darkness, moving just above that mighty flowing river, beneath the moonlight, and never leaving, was this: Isidore never stood trial. There was no time for that, in their defining who they were. The pushing to it. This burning need of them.

All those who remember still.

They let his wounds heal, behind the man-made bars of their fears. Their fear becoming hatred. Hatred, defining them, and institutionalized now, for all to see, who cared to see it.

Not many.

Not many, still.

The whispers. The accusations. He raped her. Can you imagine?

That poor little girl, Lizzy.

A monster. Who walks among us.

And it grew, until it could not be contained, and they gathered outside the jail.

He'll hang this day, and not a day later.

Just one more, this day. Once again. One more tree.

The sheriff and his deputies watching.

Lizzy coming to the window of her new home, Finn's home. Finn's father, holding her back, saying, there's nothing we can do.

And she cried. And she screamed. No.

Finn and Zander watching too.

Isidore, she screamed. Buster.

Someone please, stop this. Someone, please.

But, of course, no one did, and they hung him, from a large oak tree with its Spanish moss. He was told to step up onto the back of a pickup truck, the shocks of the truck sinking beneath the weight of him, such a man as that, and one never seen again, like him. God there, our father—his father, sitting high up in the tree, watching, and wondering, will it always be like this?

Yes, he thought, even with the coming of new gods soon. Yes, still.

And the Monkey King swung by the neck, long into the night, long past most of the people leaving. Dr. Honey asked to stay, and pronounce him dead.

Was he?

Ever?

So, said the doctor, yes.

And in the moving branches of the trees, in the quiet under the moonlight, his voice was heard, once again, saying: You are a child of God too.

For there is only love, and there is mercy.

PART NINE

I hate him.

You do?

Yes, why, don't you?

I don't know, I just miss him, and I want him to come home, still.

Well, stop that, because he's not.

You don't know, Mackenzie. He might.

Cael, listen to me. He lied. And that's what he is, a liar, and a coward. I mean, no one's even heard from him.

Maybe something happened to him, and he can't come home. Not yet. Maybe that?

Like what?

I don't know, something.

Yeah, maybe something. She looked away, and with tears in her eyes, she said, and maybe not.

They sat more, not speaking, on the bank of that mighty river, together watching the current flowing by, taking their father with it; their dreams of a life not this, the Spanish moss above them, swaying in a warm breeze.

And they wondered more, what happened, Dad, why didn't you come home, like you said you would?

Would they ever know why? They didn't know if they would, or not, in this world of theirs now, a world that would always be, just that, the real and the imagined. Sad and forever. And only that.

Isabelle looked out the window of the bus, and she thought, where are you, Finn? Be there, in Tidewater, waiting.

She closed her eyes, the bus rolling on, over the high hills, back to that place she once knew, and thought she'd never see again.

Her home, Tidewater, USA.

Independence Day. The United Christian States of America.

April 17th. A day of all days. A clear, beautiful day, with nothing but blue skies, as if He Himself had arranged it to be so.

A celebration of a sovereignty-association. A nation of God within a nation. This reconstructing of greatness; of destiny; of reaching far beyond anything ever seen before on these shores.

An execution of purity, in their beliefs, exhibited for all to see. Their pride in knowing they were right, and always would be, in these ways of God.

The unveiling of four giant crosses, one at each compass point, defining the geographical boundaries of God's nation in America. This great, born-again nation.

These United Christian States of America.

At the podium, Sterling Spalding said, destiny. Here, now, and always. By His hand to ours, and he looked down at Hunter, in a suit, standing next to him, and he took his hand in his. By His will, to ours. And he said, humble before God.

And more than a quarter million people in attendance, said, praise Jesus.

The old man, with the beautiful olive skin, rode a horse, and he stopped.

A wolf trailing him, stopped.

Ty, the young boy with the long blonde hair, trailing the wolf, stopped.

Before them, Finn—a fallen man at the side of the road.

The wolf, stretching out in the tall grass next to the road, watched the old man dismount.

The young boy, Ty, watched the old man approaching Finn, bending to one knee, and placing two fingers on Finn's neck.

He heard Him say, yes yes, I see.

The wolf closed its eyes, the old man searching through Finn's pockets. He looked at the gun on the road, and he looked back at Finn.

He opened the backpack next to Finn, and began to search through it, and as he did, he said, I once owned a farm. It wasn't much at all. Just a small thing, but so very beautiful. And when you'd ride up that long laneway, you'd cross a creek, and you'd dog leg left to get to the house. And where that laneway bent, he used his right hand to illustrate a dog leg left, there was a slaughterhouse, on the outside of the turn, for horses. Pitiful.

Flies everywhere. He held his hands up before him and indicated a space of about a foot and a half. Rats this big. It was terrible, all those horse carcasses piled up, one on top of the other, 'till you'd think the wagon was about to tip over. Headless and skinned, butchered with their hooves still on. 'Course, it wasn't too long before I took that slaughterhouse down.

He looked up the long, quiet road. Nothing moving. No wind. A perfect silence. He looked back at Finn. There was a pasture at the front of the house, and every time I'd fetch a horse, and I do mean, every single time, with any horse, over all the years I lived and worked there, I'd walk that horse up the laneway with the big willows hangin over it, well, just as soon as I'd start around that dog leg, all hell would break loose. They'd spook, rearin up and steppin back. Now why would that be? Why would a horse, years and years after I'd torn that slaughterhouse down, spook, in that very spot? Every time? Every horse?

He stood and stroked the side of his horse's head. Just think, if you were a horse, what that place must have seemed like?

He mounted his horse and looked back at Finn. I've often wondered, what if some people were like that? If they too could see beyond what was just there? And if they could, what kinda of darkness that would be? Even just a glimpse, you would think, would be enough.

He kicked the horse and started up the road. Imagine, he said, a look into the slaughterhouse of all man's time. Yes yes, just horrible. An unimaginable darkness.

The wolf lifted its head and watched the old man riding away. It stood and approached Finn. Looking around, it lowered its head and sniffed him. And then, as if satisfied with what it had found, it crouched and leaped and began to run, following the old man up the road, over the high rolling hills without trees, disappearing somewhere just beyond the farthest reaches of the midnight sun.

The bus pulled away, leaving Isabelle standing alone with her bag at the side of the road. She looked around, and she started to walk toward Tidewater. Toward Finn, who was not there.

But his kids were, and she would soon come to know this, and seek them out, and tell them, he loved them deeply, and no matter what happened, that kept him away, it was not because he did not love them. Never that.

Never that always.

Would she stay in Tidewater? With her ghosts? Those of her father? Finn?

Ghosts, she thought, that when we live long enough with them, we become them.

An inescapable, or so it seemed to her, sadness, that she was not sure she wanted to own. Thinking always, one day, he might come back.

And so, she left, choosing instead, that which was here.

Life now. As it is.

As it can be.

They sat in two straight back chairs on the broken porch of the abandoned cabin looking out at a landscape Jake remembered well.

Nothing ever happens, back there, the way you think it will. No?

No, Amanda said. Unless you're my father, then, well—nothing doesn't work out for him, does it? His will, to do as he pleases. By his design. Or, so it seems.

Jake looked at Amanda. The hell with him, and all the others like him.

It's strange though, isn't it? How that works.

I guess. But I couldn't be more disinterested in those people—those kind of people, and I hope they all rot in hell one day.

That'd be nice, wouldn't it? But I won't hold my breath.

Yeah, well, fortunately, we're not those people, and we're not there now. And I could not possibly be happier about that. Because what I want, Amanda, is to be anywhere but there.

She looked at Jake and she reached her hand out and took his into hers, and she smiled.

Not that there's anything special about here, but, at least, it's not there.

No, but Hunter is.

Yeah, I'm working on that. But we might need to give it some time first, for things to cool down.

She looked at Jake. Except, I'm not sure he shouldn't be.

Oh?

It's sad, I know, but it seems like, she paused, tears coming to her eyes, like that's where he's meant to be. His fate. What's best for him. She got up and sat on Jake's lap, and he put his arms around her. She leaned her head against his chest. What's by design, and what's not? I'll never know. And I don't know if I ever will. Or, need to.

Yeah, it's probably best that way, I would think. At least, the way things go, it seems like it.

I'd like to become, I don't know, she looked at Jake, enough. Me, without plans—without trying to become those plans. To trust in faith. The faith of us, without knowing. Of being true to that. It seems like, that's hard enough, and enough. We're here now, together. After all of this time. After all of our … individual plans, and how those worked out for us.

Jake laughs. Yeah, we really screwed things up, back then, didn't we?

Did we? Or was it our pasts that brought us together, finally?

You think?

I don't know. I think so. I mean, we weren't ready, for whatever reason, back then. But we are now. At least, I know I am. She looked at Jake. No matter what.

Yes, he said, as I am, too, no matter what, and he leaned forward and he kissed her, for there is always love under a big moon, somewhere.

That's what he hoped.

That's what she knew.

This day, now. This day, always.

In his mind, Finn wakes.

He's young, standing in a forest of tall, towering trees.

A canopy of light, and he starts to walk.

It's quiet, and it's still. Everything so perfectly quiet and perfectly still. Soon, he comes to a valley of mist, and he walks through it. He sees many young children, dressed in ragged and torn clothing, appearing, disappearing. Appearing again. Some holding silent, new born babies.

He walks more, exiting the mist, and he walks through another forest of tall trees.

He comes to a clearing where he sees Isidore, standing with his back to him, looking off somewhere else.

Lizzy was there, standing next to Isidore. She looks back at him, and she smiles.

He smiles, too, and he walks forward, standing to the other side of Isidore, and together, they stand looking at the black, scorched earth before them.

The falling, heavy gray ash of a world that once was.

Fate there, too, standing, watching, waiting.

The old man with the beautiful olive skin, smiles, and he says, Fate, my darling, I found you. I knew I would.

I always do.

CODA

In the great plaza, build specifically for this Independence Day, with its giant cross, the founding fathers of the United Christian States of America were being seated in white folding chairs.

Sterling, standing next to the Quiet Man, was being summoned. He held up his hand, as if to say, one minute, he'll be right there. Looking at Hunter, standing off to the edge of the plaza, watched by his Oath Holder minders, Sterling leaned closer to the Quiet Man, and he whispered, it won't work. I can't live with it.

The boy?

Yes.

I understand.

Good, said Sterling, see that it gets done, and he joined the others, and was seated front and center for the official portrait of this historical day.

The United Christian States of America.

In God we trust.